THE
INVITING SCHOOL
TREASURY

THE INVITING SCHOOL TREASURY

1001 Ways To Invite Student Success

William Watson Purkey

Paula Helen Stanley

SCHOLASTIC

LEADERSHIP
POLICY
RESEARCH ™

New York • Toronto • London • Auckland • Sydney

Copyright ©1994 by Scholastic Inc.

No part of this publication may be reproduced in whole or in part, or stored in a retrieval system, or transmitted in any form or by any means, electronic, mechanical, photocopying, recording, or otherwise, without permission of the publisher. For information regarding permission, write to Scholastic Inc., 555 Broadway, New York, NY 10012.

ISBN 0–590–49717–0

12 11 10 9 8 7 6 5 4 3 2 1   1 2 3 4 5 / 9

Printed in the U.S.A.

Library of Congress Cataloging-in-Publication Data

Purkey, William Watson.
   The inviting school treasury: 1024 ways to invite student success in your school/
William Watson Purkey, Paula Helen Stanley.
     p.   cm.
   Includes bibliographical references (p.) and index.
   ISBN 0–590–49717–0
   1. School environment—Handbooks, manuals, etc. 2. Classroom environment—Handbooks,
manuals, etc. 3. School management and organization—Handbooks,, manuals, etc. I. Stanley, Paula
Helen. II. Title.
LC210.P87   1994
371.2—dc20
                                                          93-34724
                                                              CIP

Designed by Joan Gazdik Gillner

Dedication

To The Student Who Will Benefit From This Book:

What is a Student?

A **student** is the most important person ever in this school...in person, on the telephone, or by mail.

A **student** is not dependent on us...we are dependent on the **student**.

A **student** is not an interruption of our work...the student is the purpose of it.

We are not doing a favor by serving the **student**...the **student** is doing us a favor by giving us the opportunity to do so.

A **student** is a person who brings us his or her desire to learn. It is our job to handle each **student** in a manner which is beneficial to the **student** and ourselves.

(Adapted by William W. Purkey from an L. L. Bean Co. poster: "What is a customer?" by J. M. Eaton.)

Table of Contents

Acknowledgements

Many of the ideas that appear in *The Inviting School Treasury* were adapted, modified, culled, and compiled from earlier suggestions that appeared in articles, monographs, and books on Invitational education. Additional ideas were given to the authors by colleagues from throughout the United States, Canada, and abroad.

While individual contributors are too vast in number (and our recordings too lax) to acknowledge each one personally, we extend our heartfelt thanks to all who contributed ideas that appear in *The Inviting School Treasury*.

You may find some of your favorite ways to invite success missing from this volume, so suggestions to the authors will be most welcome and carefully considered for a second edition. Please send your suggestions to us at the following addresses:

William Watson Purkey
Department of Counseling and
Educational Development
University of North Carolina
at Greensboro
Greensboro, NC 27412

Paula Helen Stanley
Department of Counselor
Education
Radford University
Radford, VA 24142

Introduction

Welcome to *The Inviting School Treasury*. The ideas presented here have been created, collected, culled, adapted, and compiled by the authors for over a decade. We think they represent the best in inviting school practices. You are cordially summoned to dive in and fill your pockets with over 1,000 ways to encourage academic achievement by making school the most inviting place in town.

The basis of this treasury is invitational education (Purkey & Novak, 1984; Purkey & Schmidt, 1988, 1990; Purkey & Stanley, 1991; Purkey & Strahan, 1986; Novak, 1992). Invitational education is a theory of practice designed to create a total school environment that intentionally summons people to realize their relatively boundless potential in all areas of worthwhile human activity. It addresses the global nature of school environments—the entire gestalt. Its purpose is to make learning, teaching, leading, and living a more exciting, satisfying, and enriching experience for everyone in and around schools. Its method is to offer a guiding theory, a language of transformation and a practical means to accomplish its stated purpose.

A NOTE OF CAUTION

One note of caution is necessary in applying this collection of ideas. Invitational education can easily be misunderstood, misused, or corrupted by those who have learned its techniques but not its philosophy. Invitational education is far more than a thousand clever ideas such as the ones in this book. To avoid misunderstandings, it is critical that those who seek to employ invitational education in their schools study its intellectual and ethical dimensions and continuously work to develop their understanding of its richnesss and complexity. By developing a deeper understanding of the structure of invitational education, educators can combine these thousand ideas into a seamless whole and understand how each idea works progressively to create totally inviting schools.

Proponents of invitational education are asked to delve deeply into its theoretical and ethical components. A good place to start is to read *Advancing Invitational Thinking* by John Novak (Ed.), San Francisco: Caddo Gap Press, (1992); *Inviting School Success* by William W. Purkey and John Novak, Belmont, Ca: Wadsworth Publishing Company, (1984); *Invitational Teaching, Learning and Living* by William W. Purkey and Paula Helen Stanley,

Washington, DC: National Education Association, (1991), and other articles and books on invitational education listed in the references. The term *invitational education* was chosen because the two words have special meaning. The English word *invite* is probably a derivative of the Latin word *invitare,* which means "to offer something beneficial for consideration." Translated literally, *invitare* means "to summon cordially, not to shun." The word *education* comes from the Latin word *educare,* which means "to call forth something potential or latent."

Literally, invitational education is the process by which people are cordially summoned to realize their relatively boundless potential in all areas of worthwhile human endeavor. Implict in this definition is that invitational education is an ethical process involving continuous democratic interactions among and between human beings.

Invitational education maintains that every person and everything in and around schools add to, or subtract from, the process of becoming a beneficial presence, or a lethal one, in the lives of human beings. Ideally, the factors of people, places, policies, programs, and processes should be so intentionally inviting as to create a world in which each individual is cordially summoned to develop intellectually, socially, physically, psychologically, and spiritually. This ideal served as the basic selection process for theideas considered for this book.

THE SELECTION PROCESS

Each suggestion considered for inclusion or exclusion in this treasury was evaluated on the basis of its compatibility with five basic propositions of invitational education:

1. Education should be a cooperative activity.

2. Process is as important as product.

3. People are able, valuable, and responsible and should be treated accordingly.

4. People possess untapped potential in all areas of worthwhile human endeavor.

5. Potential can best be realized by places, policies, processes, and programs specifically designed to invite development, and by people who are intentionally inviting with themselves and others personally and professionally.

In addition to the requirement of compatibility with invitational education, we included our own measuring rod in determining what should be included. Here are the questions we asked of each potential entry:

- Does the idea relate to student success in school? (Is it related to *academic achievement?*)

- Is the idea positively worded? (Does it explain what *to* do, not what *not* to do?)

- Is the idea behaviorally anchored? (Is it anchored in action?)

- Is the idea sufficiently fresh? (We eliminated many ideas that we considered over-used.)

- Does the idea support the inviting process? (We omitted hundreds of "self-esteem building" exercises because they are not the focus of this book.)

- Does the entry emphasize rewards, prizes, incentives, gifts, and the like? (We decided not to use hundreds of ideas based on competitions and rewards. There were so many ideas regarding stickers, stars, happygrams, badges, patches, buttons, ribbons, balloons, bumper stickers, and the like that these incentives could fill a book of their own. That we did not use these ideas in no way detracts from their value. They simply did not fit with the focus of this book.)

Now for some additional mechanics. This *Treasury* is organized alphabetically by subject or topic. Each of the entries is cross-referenced in an extensive reference index at the back of the book. Should a topic of interest not appear in the "Table of Contents," check the index at the back of the book. For example, "Guests" might be listed under "Visitors" or "Company" in the index. Each entry is cross-referenced.

This book will be a valuable source book for anyone who is involved with life in and around schools, including food service professionals, librarians, principals, secretaries, superintendents, teachers, counselors, custodians, consultants, supervisors, bus drivers, volunteers, students, and assorted human service professionals who care for students.

Thank you for considering these many ways to make school "the most inviting place in town."

Welcome to *The Inviting School Treasury*. There is something in this volume for everyone who lives and works in schools. These 1000-plus ways to invite school success have been culled from countless ideas suggested to or invented by the authors. We believe that you will be able to find good ideas on every page of this *Treasury*.

ACADEMIC ACHIEVEMENT

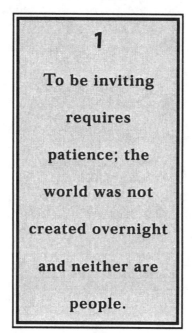

1

To be inviting

requires

patience; the

world was not

created overnight

and neither are

people.

2 Send Lessons C.O.D. It helps to organize lessons around:

    Content—appropriate, meaningful, solid
    Organization—logical, simple, visible
    Delivery—interesting, clear, energetic.

3 Stress Practice. Often teachers say to students, "All I ask you to do is your best." This is usually countered by "This is my best." A better approach is to say, "I know you can do better, so PRACTICE." By seeing students as they could be, rather than as they are, a teacher's vision becomes a student's reality.

4 Form Triads. Divide the class into groups of three, called "Triads." Ask each triad to research, obtain materials, and teach a mini-lesson on selected course content. Placing a student who is having behavior difficulties with two well-behaved peers invites new friendships, breaks down barriers, and provides role models for the rambunctious youngster.

5 Send Unconditional Invitations. Sometimes educators are guilty of sending invitations to students that suggest doubt in their ability or willingness to accept. For example, "You can do this work, Bill, if you will try." Simple declarative statements are best: "You *can do* this work, Bill."

6 Increase Odds Of Success. Students are most likely to accept the teacher's invitation to achieve academically when six conditions are present:
    1. when it is safe to try.
    2. when it is not overly demanding.
    3. when they are warmly encouraged.
    4. when they believe they can meet the teacher's expectation.
    5. when good things have resulted from accepting in the past.
    6. when they feel respected by the teacher.
The teacher influences *all* of these conditions.

7 Take Time For Commercials. Divide the class into small "film companies" and ask each company to prepare a one-minute commercial on an academic concept. Each company is invited to write, direct, and videotape its commercial for class viewing. This process invites both academic learning and student enthusiasm. It also encourages creativity.

8 Teach Something Tough. A great way to invite students to achieve academically is to teach them something that others do not know. This is particularly important when working with students labeled "slow" and placed in "special" classes. In vocabulary instruction, for example, the teacher may include a few very difficult words such as "proselytize" or "proletariat." The math teacher may teach a few tricks that even the so-called "bright" students don't know. Few things are more enhancing than special knowledge, particularly when students are trying desperately to avoid such labels as "slow learner" or "developmentally handicapped."

9 Teach Less Better. Concentrate on what is truly important in course content, and teach it well. Some teachers overwhelm students by giving too much too fast. The formula is "Teach half as much twice as well." Make sure the things taught stay taught by frequent reviews of important content.

10 Review Activities. Too often, when parents ask their children "What did you learn in school today?" the answer is "Nuthin!" To avoid this, spend the last few minutes of class each day reviewing the learning that took place during the day's activities. This is helpful to students, the teacher, *and* the parents.

11 Practice T.Q.M. Practice Total Quality Management techniques in and out of the classroom. Tell students what they are expected to learn, give them tips on *how* to go about learning, give a test to be sure they do learn, give immediate feedback, and give extra attention to students who are confused.

12 Use The Blackboard. Get in the habit of listing daily objectives on the blackboard. This keeps the lesson focused. It also saves wear and tear on the copier.

13 Maintain A Giveaway Library. Books are meant to be used. A way to encourage reading is for the teacher to read a passage or section from a favorite book, then present the book to some student as a gift. Teachers can keep a fresh stock of books on hand by visiting garage sales, flea markets, and goodwill industries. It's worth the small cost of a used book for a student to hear a teacher say, "Here is a book I want you to have and enjoy. I think it was written just for you!"

14 Start A Trading Library. Set up a small library in the classroom where students can donate books and take turns serving as librarian. Explain to students that books are meant to be used and enjoyed. The library promotes sharing, reading, and responsibility.

15 Hold A Fractions Party. Bring (or ask the class to bring) some pies, square cakes, or other goodies and invite students to recognize the differences among 3/4, 5/8, 1/2, or 1/3. (They get to eat their answers.) It will not take long for every student to learn there is a big difference between 2/3 and 1/3!

16 Post A Weekly "Stumper." For example, "How far can the QE II cruise on one gallon of gas?" (answer: 6 inches!) This will quickly send students to available almanacs, newspapers, etc. Research becomes fun!

17 Discover What's Old And New. Ask students to name the "oldest" and "newest" things in the room. (The teacher will quickly be named the "oldest" thing in the room, so be forewarned.) This search opens up all sorts of possibilities to explore the natural sciences.

18 Bring History Alive. Invite students to make a historical poster announcing special occurrences or depicting exciting events. Students can draw the posters, prepare a brief history of the event, and illustrate the event.

19 Encourage Effort. The worst effort in life is the effort that was never made. A life spent making mistakes is far greater than a life spent doing nothing. Encourage students to try. Nothing is worse than not trying. Ask: Did you try and fail? Or did you fail to try?

20 Get To Carnegie Hall. Top performers, including artists, athletes and scholars, arrived at the top because of drive and determination, *not* great natural talent. *Hard work* is the secret of extraordinary success. "How do I get to Carnegie Hall?" Answer: "Practice."

21 Watch For "Help" Signs. Watch for "I need help" signs among the students. Keep a lookout for the student who wants to learn but is having difficulty doing so. Discreetly offer to help the struggling student after class or before or after school.

22 Organize "Study Buddies." Using a *random* system, pair students together for periods of study. Have the two work together over extended periods to check on each other's progress, share concerns, and celebrate successes.

23 Encourage Cooperative Learning. One of the most exciting and innovative practices in contemporary education is pairing students of different performance levels. Insure that each student has a clear responsibility for part of the assignment.

24 Tote That Pack. Students who succeed in school are usually those who have good organizational skills. Encourage all students to obtain a backpack or other bag in which to organize their school supplies and carry them back and forth to school.

25 Point Out What's Important. Many students at all levels have difficulty in trying to figure out what is important in a class lesson and what is not. Teachers can help student learning by stating *"This is important"* when they come to critical parts of a lesson.

26 Capture Key Ideas. Write key words and important concepts on the blackboard, overhead transparency, or large newsprint during a class lecture. Ask students to "capture" these in their notebooks because they are likely to appear on future tests. This encourages vocabulary development, correct spelling, and comprehension.

27 Teach Test-Taking Methods. To improve performance on standardized tests, teach students test-taking skills. For example:

- Be alert for key words such as *always, never, none, usually, perhaps,* or *sometimes.*
- Read all choices first; sometimes the last choice is "all of the above."
- Eliminate the answers that are obviously wrong, then select from the rest.

ADMINISTRATION

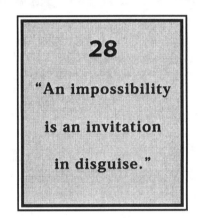

28

"An impossibility

is an invitation

in disguise."

29 Keep People Posted. Accurate information is the natural enemy of rumors. Insure prompt and accurate communication by using announcements, newsletters, memos, and bulletin boards. Even a small blackboard near the mailboxes can be used to remind folks of upcoming events. For important events, use more than one system of communication.

30 Visit The Provinces. The school administrator is responsible for the entire school, not just the office. Visit the teachers' lounge, gym, cafeteria, furnace room, shops, labs, classrooms, and school grounds frequently. Discipline is best handled before it becomes a problem. The secret is to be visible.

31 Practice Proactive Assessment. Rather than developing a spirit of "Why are you not doing more?" think in terms of "I'm glad you're here," and "We're going to make important contributions to this school." Positive attitudes are beneficial to both morale and achievement.

32 Sail On. As Columbus faced the obstacles of the uncharted Atlantic, he wrote in his log of the Pinta each evening: "This day we sailed on." Columbus's rule for administrators might be: "Get Started, Keep Going, Sail On."

33 Pat Some Backs. Give complete, full, and prompt recognition for a job well done. Too often, the only feedback faculty and staff receive is negative. Make a special effort to compliment good work.

34 Practice Pigeon Walking. When pigeons are walking they usually stop after each step or two to look around and figure out where they are going. It is a sort of refocusing. Administrators can "Pigeon Walk" by pausing from time to time to see where they are, where they've been, and where they are going.

35 Do Some Brainstorming. A valuable adage is "None of us is as smart as all of us." If the school has a problem or challenge, sometimes it helps to get a lot of heads together to find a good solution. The group should include faculty, staff, students, and parents.

36 Practice The Three P's. Promptness, Politeness, and Patience are three vital qualities of the school administrator. When callers and visitors are attended to politely, patiently, and attentively, they are in a much better position to express their needs and concerns.

37 Save Money. Keep in mind how much money invitational education can save a school:
- Improved teacher morale means lower teacher absenteeism.
- "Teaching to Pass" means fewer students retained at grade level.
- Improved student morale means lower student absenteeism.
- Happy students mean less vandalism and breakage.
- Fewer discipline problems mean increased administrative productivity.
- Fewer "grievances" mean fewer legal/management labor difficulties.

38 Keep Marching. The greatest mistake anyone can make in life is to worry continually about making mistakes. Spending one's life making mistakes is far better than spending a life doing nothing. When an effort fails, use the experience to learn and develop.

39 Practice The Four D's. When mail arrives, sort it out with the Four D's:
1. Dump it.
2. Delegate it.
3. Delay it.
4. Do it!

40 Plan A Student Forum. Plan a student forum two or three times a year. Students meet with the administration of the school and discuss their concerns about how the school works and what they are learning. Students also discuss what they perceive is working well in the school. Forums provide administrators with valuable interactions with students and open lines of communication between students and faculty.

41 Keep A Fact File. Type up a 5 × 8 card with pertinent information about each member of the faculty and staff:
- preferred name
- birthday
- age
- address
- phone
- names of family members
- items of special interest (hobbies, unusual concerns, likes, and dislikes)

Indicate each time the administrator talked with this person. Check the file from time to time and make a special effort to talk to those who may have been overlooked.

42 Maintain A "Tickler File." Develop a reminder file with a folder for each day of the month and for each of the twelve months. If something is due in December, place a note or material in that month's file. At the beginning of each month pull the monthly file and sort into specific days. Each morning, check the file first thing.

43 Follow It Up. When someone comes to a school administrator with a concern or discloses something of a personal or professional nature, it is important to follow it up later. This shows interest and commitment and takes very little time and effort.

44 Date Everything. A good habit for administrators is to date everything that comes across the desk. This includes everything sent and received. A date stamp is a must for every administrator's desk. It will save a lot of time later when someone needs the exact date of a piece of business.

45 Include Students When Possible. When decisions concerning the school are being made, it is often useful to include students on committees or task forces. This may lead to an increased sense of responsibility on the part of students who perceive themselves as important partners in the school community.

46 Choose A Project. Organize a committee to select a project for the year. For example, one goal might be winning the Inviting School Award offered by the International Alliance For Invitational Education, or transforming the physical appearance of the building or grounds.

47 Be A Greeter. A great way to start the day right is for the school administrator to stand at one of the doorways and greet students as they enter the building. If there are several entrances to the school, randomly vary the administrator's location. This takes only a few minutes and is a valuable public relations technique.

48 Stack The Boxes. Obtain a set of stacked boxes and label each box to categorize and prioritize mail and communications. Here is a good system:
MUST DO. Can't leave until this is done.
DO SOON. Needs attention.
CAN WAIT. Do it when time permits—no rush.
One additional box can be marked for the secretary to type, distribute, or whatever.

49 Log It In. It is important to log significant conversations that the administrator has with faculty, staff, students, parents, and community members. This is particularly important when the meeting takes place behind closed doors. Note the date, time, and nature of the conversation. In a large school this log is of great help in remembering the substance of meetings.

50 Listen To The Ice. Experienced woodsmen in the far north know how to listen to the ice of a frozen pond to tell how thick or thin it is. School administrators should listen to people in the school even when time is limited or when one does not feel like listening. It might prevent a dunking in ice-cold water.

51 Chase Those Grants. While not always publicized, there are usually dozens of local or statewide grant opportunities. Governments, civic groups, and private corporations all offer some sort of funding for grants. Grants are a great stimulus to institute innovations in the school.

52 Arrange "Cracker Barrel" Luncheons. Plan a regular time when the school administrator can have some quality time with a small group of students. This "cracker barrel luncheon" can give the administrator time to meet students informally and get a feeling for students who need special attention.

53 Take A Walk. Just as it is important for teachers to greet their students each day, it is vital for the school administrator to greet teachers. It takes time to walk through the building each morning, but there is no subsitute for good communication achieved through a morning greeting and brief conversations with as many teachers as possible. This is called "administration by walking around."

54 Watch Those Words. Every word in the English language has an emotional component. Work to use inviting words, rather than disinviting. For example:

Inviting Words	Disinviting Words
Opportunity	Problem
Able	Hate
Wish	Helpless
Options	Hopeless
Success	Wrong
Proud	Difficulty
Respect	Demand
Unique	Always
Capable	Failure
Trust	Impossible

55 Seek Consensus. Too often, administrators who seek to be democratic rely on a vote. This usually ends up with "winners" (majority) and "losers" (minority). To avoid this win/lose situation, work hard to seek general agreement on an issue. Consensus does not mean that everyone is happy with the decision, but simply that everyone is willing to "go along."

56 Share Responsibility. Make working together a partnership. When all parties share responsibility, a feeling of self-worth is established, which, while valuable in itself, also enhances job performance.

57 Allow Time For Deadlines. Discuss deadlines with employees, in terms of available personnel, materials, and time needed to insure completion of a task. High stress levels are associated with low performance.

58 Involve Everyone In New Procedures. If a new procedure is implemented, carefully explain and involve all concerned. Being informed gives employees a feeling of importance and reduces fear of the unfamiliar.

ADVISOR/ADVISEE PROGRAMS

59 Develop Advisor/Advisee Programs. Teachers provide guidance for students in schools, usually in an informal manner. Some schools have developed advisor/advisee programs in which teachers are assigned a few students to advise. The school may allot a certain amount of time (for example, two 30-minute periods during the week) for teachers and advisees to meet. During this time the teacher may present guidance activities on such topics as study skills, peer relationships, or wellness. Advisees also seek the assistance of teachers on a needed basis outside of the advisor/advisee meetings. The school counselor coordinates the advisor/advisee program.

60 Provide Booklets For Advisor/Advisee Programs. Teachers who participate in an advisor/advisee program benefit from booklets prepared for them on topics to be used in student advising. Counselors can provide material in the areas of peer relationships, study habits, career development, and conflict management.

61 Prepare Teachers To Facilitate. Teachers who participate in an advisor/advisee program may need to learn or "brush up" on active listening and facilitation skills. Counselors can prepare teachers to respond empathically, listen for meaning, ask open-ended questions, and help students think through a situation.

AFTER-SCHOOL ACTIVITIES

62

Life is never so

full that there is

never time for

an inviting act.

63 Plan After-School Enrichment. The school can offer a great opportunity for after-school activities. In many schools Scouts, Daisies, Brownies, and Cub Scouts meet in classrooms after school. Parks and recreation departments offer after-school activities including pottery, printmaking, cooking, health and safety, and exercise. SAT preparation courses are provided by many schools. One school even offers a ballet class sponsored by the PTA. Opening the school for after-school activities encourages public support of education.

64 Offer After-School Child-Care. Some schools provide after-school child-care. After-school care may also be offered during evening hours if the school has evening adult education classes.

65 Plan School Dances. For upper grades, a school dance can be a great builder of school spirit and school attendance. PTA/PTOs can provide chaperons and refreshments, and local disc jockeys can make an appearance and provide the music. This is a great Friday night activity and adds to the safety of young people.

66 **Host A Fund-Raising Event.** Hold a special activity (dance, auction, car wash, fair, etc.) with all profits going to a special purpose, such as computers for the school, improving the campus, or caring for a school family member with pressing needs. This brings the school family closer together.

ALUMNI

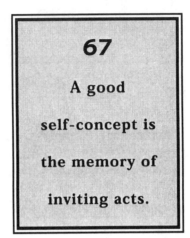

67

A good

self-concept is

the memory of

inviting acts.

68 **Celebrate Founder's Day.** Every school can celebrate its birthday. A great way to do this is to invite all alumni, faculty, and staff to come back for an assembly and open house. This is an excellent community outreach activity and is well-received by everyone who takes pride in the culture, history, and present success of the school. Don't be surprised if most of the alumni who return are the ones who have been gone from the school the longest.

69 **Arrange Alumni Treasures.** Invite famous graduates to visit classes and talk with students. Feature alumni accomplishments in a "Hall of Fame" display. Some of these alumni have relatives who may still be enrolled in the school or have significant interest in its success. These are the ones who are most likely to vote for continued support of education.

70 Hold An Alumni Day. Some schools sponsor an "Alumni Day" for former students. A dinner or lunch may be provided with present and former teachers available to interact with the alumni. Alumni Day could be held in coordination with a "Career Day." Have alumni present short descriptions of their occupations and hold question-and-answer sessions for students who are presently enrolled in the school.

ARCHIVES

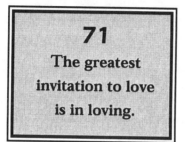

71

The greatest
invitation to love
is in loving.

72 Create A Heritage Room. A Heritage Room is an excellent way to develop historical appreciation. Find a small room somewhere in the building and include such things as the history of the school, art projects, scrapbooks, photographs, artifacts, articles, alumni activities, science projects, or special projects to be on permanent display during the year.

73 Keep A Scrapbook. Keep a school scrapbook for the year. It is easy to think of the things that happened the year before, but not as easy to think of things that happened ten years back. Scrapbooks can include such things as newspaper clippings, special bulletins, pictures of students and teachers, and special events. Scrapbooks are very popular in schools. Keep them available for families new to the school to examine. Also display them on special occasions.

74 Create A Wall Of Fame. Make a project for the year by placing historical pictures of the school on a wall at school. Pictures, paintings, pen and inks, or other drawings can be framed. If the school is named after a person, hold a celebration in honor of that person. Students will learn about the significance of the school's name and its history.

75 Plant A Time Capsule. The new year is a good time to make some resolutions. Invite students to write out some positive changes they wish for themselves. Place these statements in self-addressed envelopes and seal them away for a selected period of time. At the end of the time period, open the time capsule and distribute the letters.

ARTWORK

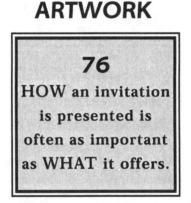

76

HOW an invitation is presented is often as important as WHAT it offers.

77 Sponsor Hallway Art Shows. Cork stripping can be placed throughout the hallways to display student work and encourage hallway decorations. To further beautify the hallways have a committee select a yearly theme for the entire school. The theme can be seasonal or on some other special topic. This makes the school attractive and is especially effective at parent/teacher conference time.

78 Hold A One-Person Art Exhibit. Whether it be a student, teacher or other talented person in the school, spotlight his or her work in some art medium for a week. Everyone benefits—the person who is honored, the students, faculty, and staff who view the art, and the people who arrange the showing.

79 **Plan A Traveling Art Show.** Give art students the opportunity to display their talents at annual city, county, or state art shows. Student artists may also display their works at a local gallery, mall, school board office showcase, or a community business. Airports, banks, and supermarkets also offer great display possibilities.

80 **Maintain A Rembrandt Board.** Younger students (and some older ones) love to give their art work to the principal. The principal will need a bulletin board for this donated work. Make sure that both the student's and teacher's names are listed on each creation so it can be returned after the showing.

81 **Honor An "Artist Of The Week."** Put one student's artwork on display in the school for a week. The student should select the artwork to be displayed and may also include his or her photograph in the display. The following week another student is selected to be artist of the week.

82 **Create Ceiling Art.** A unique approach to the appreciation of art is for students to create artwork on ceiling tiles under the supervision of the art teacher. Each design that is approved for a ceiling tile is autographed and dated by the art teacher.

83 **Publish An Artists' Magazine.** This school magazine can feature artistic, poetic, or prose creations from many, if not all, of the students in the class or school. It is fun to think up the right name for this magazine, and students take great pride in being a "published" artist.

84 **Start A Funny Paper.** On large paper (8 × 11 or larger) start a class cartoon strip. This cartoon can be added to by students and teacher. Cartoons of school experiences can help to lighten things up in the classroom.

ASSEMBLIES

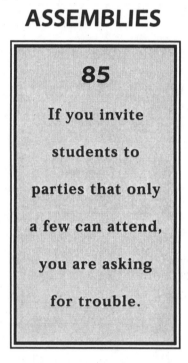

85

If you invite

students to

parties that only

a few can attend,

you are asking

for trouble.

86 **Honor Seniors Assembly.** During the last day of school for seniors, honor them with a special Awards Assembly. Scholarships, awards, certificates, and honors can be presented at this time.

87 **Provide "Motivational" Assemblies.** Design assemblies to encourage students to set goals, have high expectations for themselves, take responsibility for their own behavior, and practice moral and ethical standards. For example, presentations by TV personalities, sport stars, people with AIDS, and recovering drug users can encourage students to take responsibility for their own welfare.

88 Present A Faculty/Staff Variety Show. One of the most popular of student assemblies is a talent show provided by faculty and staff. Most schools have faculty and staff with special talents that they can share with students. If not, skits and plays performed by faculty and staff are always a hit. These assemblies are great morale boosters for both students and school professionals.

89 Spotlight Student Talent. Student talent assemblies give students the chance to "strut their stuff." All sorts of talents can be showcased, including musical groups, dance acts, readings, tumbling, monologues, skits, and other entertainment. Get as many students involved as possible.

90 Plan A Celebration. Plan a celebration assembly for the school to greet the new school year. Ask teachers, staff members, students, and parents to contribute ideas and to work toward a special program. All guests and presenters can be given a coffee mug and school button in appreciation of their support of the school.

91 Knock 'em Dead. When making a presentation at a school assembly, make it a "recess":
  Relevant
  Enjoyable
  Compact
  Energetic
  Short
  Simple

92 Double-Check Everything. Unlike singers, speakers must communicate ideas to evoke a reaction. Therefore, an ineffective mike, improper lighting, limited visibility, physical proximity, room arrangement, and even room temperature are critical. Insist on making the environment as inviting as possible.

AT-RISK STUDENTS

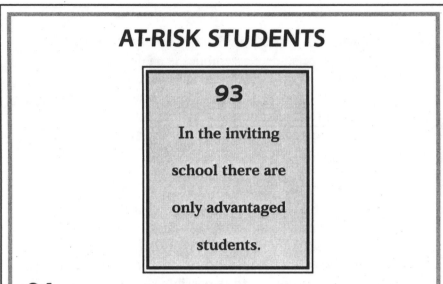

93

In the inviting

school there are

only advantaged

students.

94 Share At-Risk Ideas. Ask all the professionals in the school to keep a log or diary on useful strategies that seem to be successful with students labeled "at-risk." At the end of the year ask everyone to leave their diaries or logs with the At-Risk Committee for inclusion in a binder available to everyone.

95 Be A Guardian Angel. Keep a close eye on "at-risk" students to insure that these children are included in any breakfast or lunch programs available in the school. A discreet provision of new or clean used clothing, uniforms, or athletic equipment for those who cannot afford them is important.

96 Arrange A Field Promotion. Select a student in school whom some consider troublesome or "at-risk" and ask the student to serve as "administrative aid" to the principal for parents' night. He or she may not show up, but it's worth the gamble.

97 Insure Success For Everyone. All school recognitions should be expanded to include "at-risk" students. New categories can be developed for recognitions, such as "Most Improved" or "Extra Effort." All students should be recognized at some point.

98 **Form a SMART Committee.** (Student Management At-Risk Team). This team of administrators, teachers, guidance counselors, and social service personnel meets regularly to explore and develop successful programs, policies, and processes for working with "at-risk" students. Case studies are considered and special remediation efforts are planned and implemented to reach "at-risk" students before they drop out.

99 **Adopt-A-Student.** Implement a "buddy system" in the school in which a school professional becomes a special mentor for each "at-risk" student. These caring "buddies" hold private conferences with the student, function as a special friend, contact the student immediately when he or she is absent from school, and are available to others for consultation regarding the student's progress.

100 **Offer School Survival Training.** Create a special "mini-course" for "at-risk" kids called "How to survive in school." This would include (a) how to listen effectively, (b) how to take good notes, (c) how to get along with others, (d) how to figure out what a teacher really wants, (e) what to do when the assignment can't be completed, and (f) how to manage conflict. After this course is developed and tried with "at-risk" children, see whether or not it would be a good idea to teach this course to every student.

101 **Bring On The Tutors.** Arrange special tutorial services or classes for students in need of extra help while preparing for state functional tests. It helps to assign at-risk students to one teacher who takes primary responsibility for reteaching a hard-to-grasp skill. Volunteers and peer helpers are also valuable resources.

102 Hire Community Outreach Coordinators.

These coordinators work with migrant, disrupted, or homeless families in obtaining local, state, and federal services to which they may be entitled. They can provide mini-workshops for the parents on the importance of health care and school responsibilities. A special role is to keep in contact with homeless shelters so that communications regarding the welfare of children can be facilitated.

103 Provide Equal Access.

Many "at-risk" students cannot afford academic materials (pencils, pens, notebooks, calculators, etc.) necessary to become a part of school academic life. Having access to this material opens doors for those "at-risk" students who might otherwise fade into the woodwork. Contributions from businesses can help in providing "at-risk" students a chance to participate. Make sure these materials are available when school starts and replenish them during the year for mid-year new students.

104 Create An At-Risk Policy.

Develop an at-risk policy so that all teachers and staff are aware of what needs to be done to facilitate the growth and learning of "at-risk" students. Some faculty meetings may be devoted to the topic of "at-risk" students: how to identify who they are and how to work with them. A key focus is to encourage the involvement of these students in all school activities.

105 Be A "Principal" Contact.

The school principal can contact students who are "at-risk" academically to show his or her interest in their grades. Students may be invited to the principal's office for a visit during which time the principal expresses his or her interest in the student's success. This is not the time for lectures or discipline but an opportunity for the principal to communicate his or her concern for the student's success in school.

106 Recognize The Suffering Child. Not all suffering students are "at-risk," but here are some telltale signs of a disinvited student:

- Studying one's shoes.
- Eyes that don't sparkle.
- Missing school.
- Hiding behind a book.
- Being tardy.
- Sleeping in class.
- Keeping to oneself
- Wringing one's hands.
- Test paper face down.
- Slumping shoulders.
- Failing grades.
- Neglected appearance.

When a student sends signals of being disinvited, let the student know that there are those who care and are willing to listen.

107 Start An Advisor/Advisee Program. Appointing an advisor for every student from middle school onward insures that every student is known well by at least one professional in the school. This program can include conferences on school adjustment, academic survival, study skills, time management, and interpersonal relationships.

108 Be Persistent. It is vital that teachers not give up on students. Invite more than once. Some students, particularly those at-risk, turn down the school's invitations the first time to see if they are really sincere. Be a bulldog in inviting students to realize their potential.

109 Emphasize Success. Rather than emphasizing programs that advocate punishment for dropping out of school, emphasize the advantages of staying in school, and make sure there *are* immediate advantages and immediate rewards.

110 Arrange One-On-One Tutoring. Get ahead of future problems by providing early, intensive, and immediate one-on-one tutoring for students who are falling behind in classroom skills. Try to find a way to use certified teachers for this critical early period of schooling for "at-risk" students.

111 **Encourage Higher Order Thinking Skills (HOTS).** When working with "at-risk" students, encourage their general thinking ability by arranging for "stimulating dinner table conversation" in the classroom. The HOTS Program was developed at the University of Arizona School of Education, Tucson, AZ 85721. Contact HOTS for details.

112 **Give Them The Best.** To bring "at-risk" students up to speed, give them instruction that is enriched, engaging, active, and interdisciplinary. In fact, give them instruction like that given to gifted classes.

113 **Start A "Cities in Schools" (CIS) Program.** The Cities in Schools Project encourages the repositioning of social service staff in all fields (health, recreation, counseling, financial, legal, and employment) directly in the school. Often the CIS Program will provide support for the entire family to keep an "at-risk" child in school. For information, call CIS in Raleigh, NC. (919) 832–2700.

ATTENDANCE

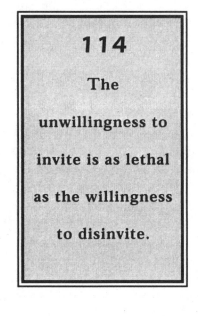

114

The

unwillingness to

invite is as lethal

as the willingness

to disinvite.

115 **Take To The Airways.** One Maryland high school operates its own FM radio station. Each day at 11:30 a.m. the station announces the day's absentees so parents may find out if their child is in the building that day. It is staffed by students five days a week, including evenings. Music from the station plays in the cafeteria during lunch shifts.

116 **Hold Happy Weekend Drawings.** Each Friday one student's name is drawn at random. If the student is in school that day and has not missed a school day that week, he or she wins a prize. The school cooperates with local businesses to provide prizes.

117 **Have An Attendance Contest.** Hold a contest between classes each grading period. Classes compete for the highest percentage of attendance, and the winning classroom wins a prize and is recognized during an assembly program. Awards and recognitions are also made to the "Most Improved" class.

118 **Give Perfect Attendance Awards.** Most schools have a Perfect Attendance Award which is given out at the end of the year. However, Perfect Attendance Awards can also be given out at the end of each grading period. Although these awards are normally given in the classrooms, they can also be announced via a bulletin board, a listing in the newsletter, over a P.A. system, or in other ways. Students will begin to take pride in being at school every day.

119 **Encourage Faculty Attendance.** The principal sends a complimentary letter to everyone on the staff who has exceptional attendance through a particular time period. Some school committees arrange a drawing (dinner for two) from a pool of those teachers who have perfect attendance over a grading period.

120 **Welcome Folks Back.** When someone in the school family has been absent, be sure to ask how he or she is feeling the first day back at school. It is important to feel missed.

121 **Demonstrate Care.** When a student misses school, make a serious attempt to find out why. Take time to phone and keep phoning until his or her attendance improves. It is vital to contact absent students each and every time they miss school. Try to talk directly to the student. If the student cannot be reached, leave a message or talk with a relative.

122 **Show Team Concern.** In schools that are lucky to have academic teams, it is helpful to call a meeting between the team and a student who returns from an absence of a week or more regardless of the reason. The team can warmly welcome the student back and create a plan for making up missed work.

123 **Send A "Welcome Back" Note.** Often professionals think to send a "get well" card to colleagues and students when they are ill. It is doubly appreciated when professionals think to send a simple "welcome back" note when the colleague or student returns.

124 **Have The Principal Call.** Any day away from school may earn a personal call from the principal. The principal expresses concern with the absence and offers a clear reminder that the student has been missed. It is usually not possible for the principal to make all the calls, but a few calls each morning will get the word out that the leadership of the school cares about students and their attendance.

125 **Practice Attendance SUCCESS.** The Attendance Challenge can be mounted on a hallway bulletin board. The names of all SUCCESS students are posted. To keep their names up, students must miss no more than two days per month. Names are removed as students miss three days or more. At the end of the month, the names still listed are dropped into a hat, and one name per grade level is chosen. Those students receive prizes or special recognition and the Challenge begins anew.

AUDIOVISUALS

126

Invitations are

like letters; they

need to be

opened, read, and

responded to.

127 Use The Opaque. An underutilized audiovisual aid in most schools is the opaque projector. With this simple machine, teachers can reproduce almost any drawing or photograph in almost any larger size. An entire wall can be filled with a map of Africa or a diagram of how a bill goes through Congress. An opaque projector, large white paper, and students with magic markers who trace the projected drawing can brighten the learning environment.

128 Give The Copy Machine A Rest. Select one day a week, or one week a month, to be a schoolwide "Be Kind to the Xerox machine" or "Save the Ditto" celebration. Encourage everyone in the school to boycott the use of copying for the one day or week. Alternative approaches, such as the use of chalk boards, can be encouraged. This will save the school a lot of money, not to mention a few trees.

AVERAGE STUDENTS

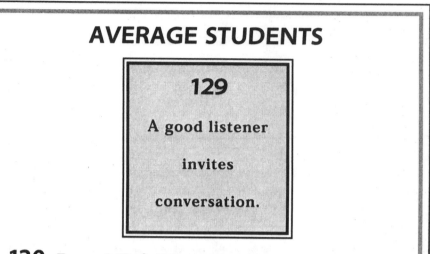

129

A good listener

invites

conversation.

130 Form A Task Force. There are many average students who tend to "fade into the woodwork." They neither cause trouble in the classroom, nor stand out because of their accomplishments. Yet these average students, with a little encourage-ment, can make significant contributions. Form a "Task Force on the Average Child" and see what the school can do to spotlight these students.

131 Invite A Triad For Lunch. Towards the beginning of the school year, have teachers arrange trade-offs to cover each other's lunch periods and free up the lunch period for two weeks. Each day that teacher chooses three students for a special luncheon invitation. Having lunch with three students each day is an excellent way to get to know students at a more personal level, particularly the "average" students who can so easily be overlooked.

132 Celebrate Skills. Students who elect to study practical skills such as business, construction, or auto mechanics are sometimes overlooked. These skilled students can make major contributions to the school, such as working on school projects, repairing student and faculty automobiles, or building projects on campus. This invites respect for everyone in the school.

133 Take A Poll. Ask students "What would you like to learn to do?" Planning and conducting mini-course electives for once-a-week sessions can help to involve average students in school activities. Learning Oriental cooking or martial arts can be a great entree to academic subject matter.

134 Hold Comprehensive Career Days. When organizing a career day for students in the school, be sure to include individuals who represent the career interests of all students. Along with inviting doctors, lawyers, and teachers, include individuals who hold positions in technical fields or who learned their skill (i.e., carpentry, bricklaying) through apprenticeship training.

BANNERS

135

If you invite your full potential, you'll throw the biggest party you've ever attended.

136 Have A Banner Year. Banners are always an eye-catching and spirit-invoking addition to any school. Students can design a grade banner or a school banner, principals can award attendance banners to classrooms, and welcome banners can be placed in the lobby or at the school entrance. For special occasions, students can initial their banners.

BIRTHDAYS

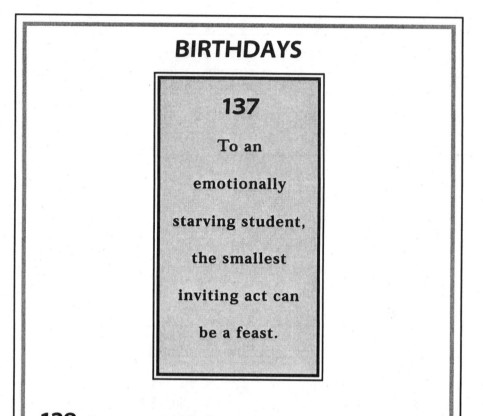

137

To an

emotionally

starving student,

the smallest

inviting act can

be a feast.

138 Present Birthday Roses. The Parent-Teacher Association can send an appreciation rose/flower to each staff member on his/her birthday to say "We Care." It demonstrates that faculty and staff are appreciated.

139 Prepare A "Birthday Box." For the busy educator, a "Birthday Box" can be prepared during the summer months. The box contains small wrapped gifts which are attractively decorated. The "Birthday Child" chooses a wrapped gift from the box for his or her own. On the last day of school, students with summer birthdays get to choose a wrapped gift.

140 Create A Birthday Calendar. Put out a monthly calendar with the birthdays of all the students in the school. Include teachers, aides, and all support staff. It gives teachers an opportunity to express a happy birthday to students in the school and to keep track of those who are having birthdays in their classroom.

141 Celebrate Birthdays. Perhaps the dining room staff can prepare a big sheet cake once a week or month for students whose birthdays fall during that period. This could be followed by announcing student birthdays over the school P.A. and a brief recording of "Happy Birthday." Be sure to include historic figures as well (Martin Luther King, Jr., George Washington, Abraham Lincoln, etc.).

142 Have Birthday Sponsors. Many children in elementary school have a class birthday party. Most often, the parent brings in the cake and the other refreshments. Seek sponsors for homeless students' birthday parties so that they are not left out.

143 Wish Happy Summer Birthdays. Sometimes people in schools who have summer birthdays get neglected. To avoid this, on the last day of school have all summer birthday people stand while everyone sings "Happy Birthday" to them.

144 Recognize School Employees. Many principals around the country give birthday cards to students, but very few give birthday cards to faculty and staff. This special recognition by the principal of the faculty and staff is well deserved. It is worth the time and effort to jot a note on a card for this special day.

145 Run A Birthday Quiz. Run a birthday quiz on the first day in the classroom. Challenge the class by commenting that there are no two people in the class with the same birthdate. Find a student with good handwriting and designate him/her as the recorder of all birthdays. If none of the birthdays match, give students two no home-work days! This is a fun, quick way of getting all of their birthdates without hassling the school secretary. When a birthday does come up, don't announce it in front of the class, but quietly put a card on the student's desk.

146 Celebrate The School's Birthday. When was the last time that the school celebrated the birthday of the person for whom it was named? This celebration can be a real educational experience. Faculty and staff may be surprised at how many students do not have the slightest idea of the origin of the school's name. This may go for the faculty and staff as well.

147 Send A Personal Greeting. Birthdays of students, faculty, and staff should be recognized with a personal greeting. Anniversaries, special holidays, other special events and noteworthy achievements can also be given special notice. For some people this simple gesture can make their day!

148 Recognize Monthly Birthdays. One faculty meeting a month can be used to celebrate the birthdays of faculty and staff members whose birthdays fall during the month. Dining room staff or parent volunteers might provide a cake large enough for the faculty.

149 Send Congratulation Cards. Birth congratulations cards can be sent to new parents in the community along with a list of available childrearing books and parenting materials that are available in the school media center.

150 Present A Birthday Cupcake. Ask the food service professionals in the school (or room parents or volunteers) to prepare cupcakes to present to students on their birthdays. This can be accompanied by singing "Happy Birthday." In June, cupcakes are given to everyone who has a summer birthday.

151 Float A Birthday Balloon. Each student's birthday can be written on a balloon with a pencil taped to it. The principal gives each child a birthday balloon. Summer birthdays can be celebrated on the last day of school.

BULLETIN BOARDS

152

Doing for others

what they can do

for themselves

can be

disinviting.

153 Use The Pinking Shears. Pinking shears can be used to cut out some of the more beautiful pictures and messages written on holiday cards. These pictures and messages can be used to decorate bulletin boards for all occasions or used as beautiful note cards.

154 Hold A Guess Who Contest. Create a bulletin board displaying teachers' childhood pictures along with little known facts, but without the teacher's name—then, guess who? Students love to learn more about their teachers.

155 Keep An Up-To-Date Bulletin Board. It is vital to insure prompt and accurate communications among faculty and staff. Keeping people posted reduces rumors and improves morale. An up-to-date bulletin board near the mailboxes helps keep people informed. This bulletin board can also be used to provide "Pocket Idea" teaching tips and to recognize new staff, including substitutes.

156 Promote Scholarship. Sometimes faculty and student bulletin boards are lacking in items of a scholarly nature. Take time to post articles, reports, and papers of an academic nature on school bulletin boards. Create bulletin boards which salute and encourage scholarship.

157 Hang A Munchkin Bulletin Board. For younger children, a child-sized bulletin board hung at their eye level is appreciated. These bright, up-to-date, and informative bulletin boards add to learning and the attractiveness of a classroom or hallway.

158 Mount A Bathroom Bulletin Board. Develop a rotating display of thoughts, suggestions, and funny and clever ideas and mount them on a small bulletin board in the teachers' bathrooms. What better reading material in rooms all teachers use!

159 Float The Bulletin Board. Obtain a large sheet of styrofoam. Place messages on it using mounted paper letters. Next, string several helium balloons to the styrofoam bulletin board. The result is a floating bulletin board that travels around the school, popping up at unexpected places. Students of all ages are remarkably gentle with this new medium.

160 Design Interactive Bulletin Boards. After a few days, a bulletin board becomes just another wall fixture, unnoticed by students. But what if it is changed often? A mystery word puzzle, for example, or a "guess this place" feature taken from a travel article in the Sunday paper, could be adapted for use on a bulletin board. Each morning's "unveiling" of the day's feature would prompt attention and spark interest in students.

161 Create An Award Bulletin Board. Develop bulletin boards to feature photos of the Citizen of the Month, Happy Birthday signs, Writers of the Month, Most Improved Students, or Math Wiz. The possibilities are many.

162 Have Students Design Bulletin Boards. Students can be encouraged to design bulletin boards for the hallways or classrooms. This is a good way to enhance cooperation and encourage creativity. If students design a bulletin board to display student work, let them choose which work they would like to display.

163 Use Mind Stretchers. Place a weekly mind stretcher on the classroom bulletin board. Start off Monday by taking a few minutes to review the questions on the board and on Friday check the answers. Give special prizes to students who answer correctly.

BUSES

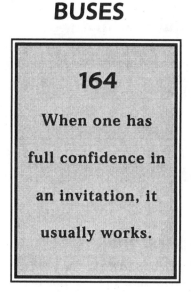

164

When one has

full confidence in

an invitation, it

usually works.

165 Do Professional Patch-Up. Torn bus seats with tape over them often lead to more torn seats. A professional patching kit works much better than tape. Catching damage early prevents the spread of further damage.

166 Greet The Morning. With each school day the bus driver can make it a point to say "Good Morning" to each student as he or she steps on the bus, and each afternoon say "So long, see you tomorrow" as each student departs for home. This habit invites a good feeling in everyone, including the driver, who is the first school professional the student sees in the morning and the last one each afternoon.

167 Look Sharp. Driving a school bus is a professional responsibility and drivers should look the part. A metal name tag for each school bus driver, coupled with a neat and well-groomed appearance, identifies drivers as professionals and encourages good behavior by students.

168 Make the Bus Inviting. A little bulletin board, some happy music, a few decorations, a smiley face, an animal cutout, a design, or the like can invite students to feel: "This is our bus. The driver takes pride in it, and so will we."

169 Set An Example. "Please" and "Thank You" are magic words. When the driver shows respect for the riders, it is likely that riders will begin to respect the driver. Civility and courtesy are critical in operating a bus.

170 Practice Cooperation. Above everything else, driving a bus is a cooperative act. Without cooperation from other drivers, riders, and the public, driving a bus would be almost impossible. Encourage cooperation by being cooperative.

171 Express Concern. When someone is ill or misses the bus, a special comment from the driver to the student when he or she returns can be a most caring and thoughtful act.

172 Practice Preventive Maintenance. Don't wait until the bus breaks down to take care of problems. A little trash can or two on the bus can be helpful in teaching students good behavior.

173 Keep The Bus Clean. Whether they admit it or not, most students enjoy riding in a clean bus. Keep the bus clean, and encourage students to help.

174 Develop Bus Spirit. At the beginning of the school year invite riders to decide upon a nickname for the bus. By using the same techniques as an athletic team, a group of riders and the driver can develop a real team spirit.

175 Divide The Routes. While this is not always possible, buses can be made more inviting if they are smaller and have shorter routes. Having different-sized buses and routes can benefit everyone as well as giving added flexibility to the school system.

176 Arrange A Late Bus Run. Many normal school days end around 3:30 p.m. Try to arrange several late buses that can depart from the school around 5:30 p.m. to allow students who are involved in extracurricular activities to get home.

177 Hold A Bus Driver Day. Have a special day in the school year to recognize bus drivers. It does not have to be a large extravagant affair, but the recognition will go a long way in identifying the vital role these support staff play in school. Just having them come in for lunch and recognizing them will suffice. Remember, the bus driver is the first person to see the students after they leave home. The tone they set is very important to the school.

178 Enrich The Training Program. In addition to the usual bus driver training programs that cover safety, maintenance, legal requirements, and the like, include such topics as "conflict resolution," "stress management," "interpersonal relationships," and "driver self-concept." These address the human side of driving a bus.

CAFETERIA

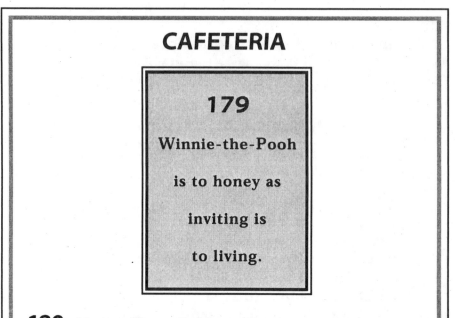

179

Winnie-the-Pooh

is to honey as

inviting is

to living.

180 **Name That Café.** Consider changing the name of the school cafeteria. One school always refers to the cafeteria as "The Dining Room." Another school has renamed its cafeteria the "Luncheon Theater." Changing the name is a great way to change perceptions and to create a more inviting place to eat.

181 **Hold Taste Tests.** Students can help judge cafeteria food on a regular basis. This will allow students and food service staff to get better acquainted, will encourage the students to see how the kitchen operates, and most importantly, will function as a source of student input.

182 **Hang Some Awnings.** Few things will make a school cafeteria come alive as effectively as hanging awnings over the doors to the serving lines. These devices, using the school colors inside the cafeteria, will brighten the entire dining area.

183 **Reduce Line Time.** Develop a flexible scheduling plan that will permit faculty, staff, and students to avoid long lines in the cafeteria. Time in school is too valuable to spend in line. Time spent on learning tasks is one of the most important ingredients in student success in school. A fast line will also encourage teachers to wait their turns in the cafeteria line.

184 Flex The Lunch Period. A flexible lunch room schedule allows students a choice as to what time they wish to go to lunch. As they go to lunch in small groups, new friendships are formed, and long cafeteria lines are avoided. This also saves valuable student learning time.

185 Celebrate National School Lunch Week. This is a good time to host parents. A special program can promote the school lunch program and give parents an opportunity to have lunch with their children.

186 Whet The Appetite. Attractive menus can be placed in the newspapers, announced on television, mounted on bulletin boards and announced with the morning P.A. news.

187 Give Some Choices. It seems wasteful to give each person the same amount of the same food. Find ways to allow students to have choices. With planning, it can be done!

188 Remember The Basics. Consider the food characteristics of color, texture, consistency, flavor combination, shape, and method of preparation. Make sure the combinations on the menu make an attractive, pleasing, and wholesome meal.

189 Practice Variety. Offering the same foods over and over is one of the most common faults in menu planning. Experiment, use foods that are in season, and take a chance!

190 Consider Appearances. Appearance alone can be changed by the garnishes and condiments used with food. Try something different.

191 Wear Colorful Uniforms. Everyone is familiar with the white outfits worn by most food-service professionals. But why not pastels once in a while? Also, whatever the uniform of the day might be, it can be accented for special times such as Christmas, Halloween, and Thanksgiving. An attractive apron can do wonders for the most sterile-looking white uniform.

192 Greet Guests. Have at least one food-service professional communicate a friendly greeting to each student as he or she moves down the cafeteria line. And do not forget a thank you at the cash end. A friendly word and smile from each food-service professional can add to the flavor of any meal.

193 Organize A Kitchen Learning Center. Many classes can benefit from visiting the kitchen and learning about food preparation procedures. This is also a good way to teach nutrition and sanitation. In high schools a visit can be used to provide special training for students interested in becoming a food-service professional. Students can organize student food-service professional clubs and function as cashiers, typists, cooks, clerks, and servers through food-service clubs or special classes.

194 Arrange Trim Line Specials. The cafeteria can offer special combination of low-calorie plates for weight-conscious members of the school family. It is also helpful to post caloric information on entrees and other items being served, along with nutrition education tidbits.

195 Play Cafeteria Music. To encourage students to keep the dining environment quieter, music can be played at a reasonable volume during lunch. Explain to students that if the music can't be heard, voices are too loud.

196 Plan An Old-Fashioned Barbecue. Have a barbecue for students once or twice a year. Work out an arrangement with food-service professionals to have hamburgers or veggieburgers cooked outside. This can be done by faculty, staff, or parent volunteers. Have the principal serve as honorary chief cook. Invite parents and have the lunch period out on the playground. Even though this takes a considerable amount of planning, the PR among the food-service professionals, faculty, staff, students, and families is outstanding. Students enjoy it, and the lunch count goes up considerably on this special day.

197 Create A Homey Atmosphere. Attractive hanging baskets and other plants make any cafeteria come alive. They also create a homey atmosphere in the cafeteria. Students, parents, or community volunteers can help with their care.

198 Provide Comfortable Seating. Seating arrangements in the dining area can have a definite effect on atmosphere. Make sure there is adequate space between tables. It is recommended that there be eighteen inches between chair backs when diners are seated. Break up long cafeteria-style tables into six-person units.

199 Encourage Wall Flowers. Because the dining area is a place where much socializing takes place, it is important to paint the walls with bright colors and decorate them with student art work, samples of student projects, and recognition of student achievement. This cuts down on the possibility of food fights.

200 Offer A Wide Variety. Rearrange the dining area so that a good selection of food items can be offered. One line could serve the daily entree while another offers soup, sandwiches, or salads. A la carte items can be made available.

201 Hold A Cafeteria Lunch Day. Invite new parents to have lunch at the school on a certain day. Allow the cafeteria staff to make appropriate decisions and invite as many teachers as possible to greet the parents.

202 Celebrate Talent. Invite the band, choir, or orchestra to perform during lunch time. This benefits both the quality of the luncheon experience and the young performers.

CALENDAR

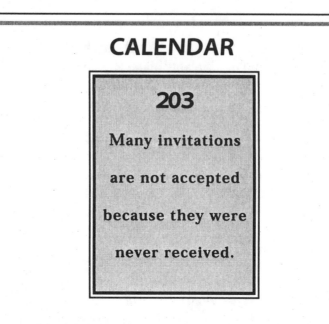

203

Many invitations

are not accepted

because they were

never received.

204 **Maintain A School Calendar.** Use a school calendar to provide students, faculty, staff, parents, and community leaders with dates for upcoming events. The calendar can be posted throughout the school as well as at locations within the community.

205 **Obtain The Inviting School Calendar.** The Alliance For Invitational Education publishes a yearly calendar with a clever idea for each day of the school year. Calendars may be ordered from the Alliance For Invitational Education, c/o School of Education, University of North Carolina at Greensboro, Greensboro, NC 27412.

206 **Planning Calendars.** Provide faculty and staff with calendars they can use for planning—as members of academic teams or individually. Better yet, ask for input from faculty and staff about the kind of calendar they would like to have.

CLASSROOM LAYOUT

207

Inviting can be

easily corrupted

by those who

learn its

technique but not

its philosophy.

208 Brighten The Classroom. Fight drabness and dreariness as much as possible. Even lining up the shades, arranging the chairs in an attractive fashion, and asking for needed repairs (including a fresh coat of paint) can make a happy difference in any classroom.

209 Alter The Layout. No matter how attractive they are, school decorations and layout eventually get stale. Change things around periodically, and be sure to ask those who share school space to assist in the planning and rearranging. A change in layout can result in a change in outlook.

210 Hang Live Plants. Attractive hanging baskets or plants on stands around the classroom improve the classroom environment. Ask groups of students to help care for them.

211 Use Floor Furniture. Almost everyone enjoys places to pause and take stock. The floor is a fine place to do this. Think of the floor as a piece of furniture. Provide big stuffed pillows, or invite each student to bring in one or two carpet squares. The class can arrange the squares according to its own taste, and then fasten to the floor. The carpet cuts down on noise, makes the room cozier, and provides a fine place for storytelling, particularly by a student visitor from a higher grade.

212 Rearrange The Furniture. Regardless of the age of the building, classrooms can be made much more inviting physically. One way to do this is to rearrange the desks and chairs from time to time. There are many designs besides straight lines. More students will feel included as the teacher rearranges their location in the classroom.

213 Take A U-Turn. Arrange desks in a "U" design so that each student has a front row seat. "Hide" the teacher's desk in the corner.

214 Form Clusters. Invite students to interact by arranging desks in clusters or groups. Proximity to friends promotes relating and learning when done correctly. This is particularly helpful in cooperative learning activities.

215 Create Attractive Classroom Doors. Teachers can welcome students into their classrooms by placing student's names in designs on the classroom door. Names can give each student a feeling of belonging: "This is my classroom. My name is on the door."

216 Hang Magic Mirrors. Obtain a full-length, shatterproof mirror and place it somewhere in the classroom so students can see themselves as they pass by. This promotes neatness and grooming among young people.

217 Build A Loft. Children love snug places and few places are as comfortable as a loft built across one end of the classroom. (Groups of parents can help with construction.) A loft gives more classroom space, and makes a fine corner for small group meetings or even plays. Sometimes carpet companies will donate remnants for covering the floor and steps. Be sure to have the loft checked for safety.

218 Provide Private Space. This is especially important if students share desks or change classrooms throughout the day. Even the smallest private storage space is sufficient for personal possessions. One teacher made personal storage spaces out of stacked tile tubing.

219 Rotate Seating. Rotate the seating pattern of the classroom as often as convenient so students "get to know" a variety of other students. This change also offers students the

220 Check The Lighting. Is the lighting in the classroom fully adequate? If not, perhaps the PTA/PTO can help by providing Venetian blinds, improving lighting, or finding other ways to brighten the classroom.

221 Keep It Clean. Research findings indicate that when educators and students work together to keep the classroom neat and clean, the amount of graffiti and vandalism throughout the entire school is reduced significantly.

222 Outdoor Classroom. Is there an open area in the center of the school? If so, it can be turned into a wonderful outdoor classroom. By adding benches and imagination, one can create a delightful learning environment for students of all ages. The site also can be used for student-teacher conferences.

223 Paint The Locker Room. A highly successful coach in Pennsylvania argues that the best way to have a winning football season is to paint the locker room. Perhaps the same is true for having a winning season in classrooms. Few things can make such an immediate improvement as a fresh coat of paint. Teachers teach better and students learn better in an inviting physical environment.

224 Attend To The Small Touches. Here are a dozen indicators of an inviting school:

Pleasant smells	Comfortable temperature
Lots of books	Bird feeders
Sunny rooms	Good ventilation
Flowers on desks	Living green plants
Matching colors	Positively worded signs
Clean windows	Attractive student displays

225 Beware Of Disinvites. Here are items that make schools unpleasant:

Full trash cans	Peeling paint and plaster
Harsh lighting	Dusty, cobwebby shelves
Excessive noise	Litter on floor
Bare walls	Torn, uneven shades and blinds
Straight rows in classrooms	Cluttered desk
	Frowning teachers
Broken furniture	Graffiti

CLASSROOM MANAGEMENT

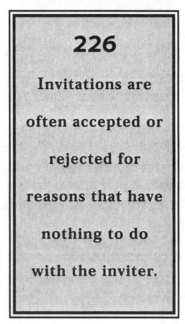

226

Invitations are

often accepted or

rejected for

reasons that have

nothing to do

with the inviter.

227 Remember The Jello Principle. The classroom and everybody in it is like one big bowl of jello: touch it anywhere and the whole thing jiggles. Everything is connected to everything else. Understanding the jello principle helps the teacher to remember that everything—temperature, time of day, color of walls, etc., adds to or subtracts from positive classroom management. Efforts to make the classroom more inviting improve the behavior of students.

228 Check The Class Pulse. Look around the classroom and observe student activity and energy levels. What is in the air? Is something special needed to get students focused on class material? Monitor the mood and energy level of students to determine the best thing to do at this moment to get students involved in learning.

229 Be Clear. To encourage good behavior, make rules that are brief, clear, and simple. Give detailed instructions describing the desired procedures. Along with clear rules, give reasons why the rules are important. Explain that these are "our" specific expected behaviors for this class.

230 Develop Linebackers' Eyes. Successful teachers are able to meet the needs of individual students while continuing a group activity. This means answering the questions of one student while continuing the group lesson. The secret is maintaining good eye contact with both the individual student and the group.

231 Try A Two-For-One. Some students need more than their "share" of attention and support. In such cases, try to find ways to meet their needs. For example, when extra textbooks are available, give certain students two copies (one for home and one for school). Another example of this principle is to assign an active student two desks (where space permits), so that he or she can move back and forth when restlessness sets in.

CLUBS

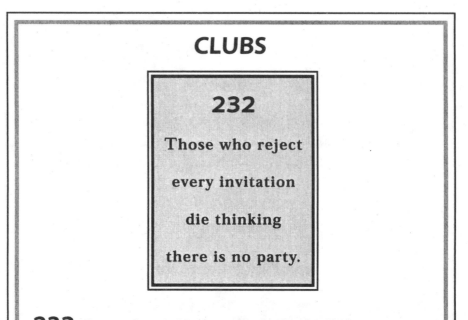

232

Those who reject

every invitation

die thinking

there is no party.

233 **Organize A Human Relations Club.** An important way to encourage cultural harmony in the school is to form a human relations group. Admission to the club is gained through writing an essay on human relations. Members are given training in conflict management and group mediation to help themselves and others solve issues and disputes before the issues become a major problem in the school.

234 **Bring On The Projectors.** An audiovisual club can be the most active and useful club in any school. Students quickly become more skillful than educators in the operation of audiovisual equipment.

235 **Form Peer Mediation Clubs.** Many small problems can be solved before they become large problems by teaching students how to mediate conflicts among peers.

236 **Involve Parents In Clubs.** Ask parents about their talents and hobbies. Questionnaires or surveys can be used for this purpose. Parents may help sponsor or work with clubs in which they have talents or skills to offer. For example, a parent with the ability to square dance might sponsor a club for students interested in this type of dance. A parent who is interested in astronomy may help with an astronomy club at school.

237 **Encourage Special Interest Clubs.** Help form and sponsor special interest groups such as an academic subject club, a bike-riding club (for those who bike to school), a jogging club (before school, at lunch, or after school), an audiovisual club (for media-oriented students), a science club for amateur astronomers, geologists, environmentalists, or a collectors club (stamps, coins, baseball cards, or whatever). The possibilities are limitless. Clubs encourage school attendance and involvement.

COMMUNITY OUTREACH

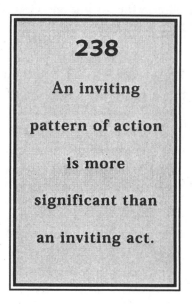

238

An inviting

pattern of action

is more

significant than

an inviting act.

239 **Hold A Breakfast For Realtors.** Most realtors are too busy to attend lunches, or too tired for dinners, but an early breakfast is always welcome. Invite all the local realtors to a breakfast and arrange a brief tour of the building or a short presentation by faculty or students regarding some special program or activity. Realtors will find this information valuable when working with house-hunting families.

240 Prepare Packets. Realtors are usually the first to make contact with people moving into the community. Provide local realtors with attractive packets of information about schools that can be shared with house-hunting families. One of the first questions asked of realtors is "What are the schools like?" Prepare the realtors by equipping them with powerful packets!

241 Welcome The Babies. Ask teachers and staff to keep the principal's office informed about the birth of a brother or sister. Follow this up with a special little card that says something like "Welcome to this bright and beautiful world. We will be looking forward to having you in our school in a few years."

242 Meet In Local Establishments. One of the best community outreach activities is for educators to hold their meetings in local businesses. Many businesses have a meeting room which could be made available to educators. Beyond the public relations benefit, educators might pick up some valuable tips on management techniques. Also, local restaurants with banquet rooms appreciate school business.

243 Let The Good News Roll. It is never a question of whether or not the schools have public relations; it is a question of what kind. Take every opportunity to let the public learn about schools, including ordering extra copies of the yearbook for distribution to all community doctor and dentist offices, sending school newsletters to community and business leaders, and arranging for visits from local news media to spotlight school activities.

244 Hold An Open House. Let the community know of the school's success by holding a neighborhood open house. An important aspect of the open house is to ask school parents to bring neighbors who do not have children in school to visit the school. Special invitations can be sent to all local business, civic, and religious organizations. This lets a large audience learn about the many good things happening in schools.

245 **Establish A Speakers Bureau.** Establish a list of educators who are willing to speak to community groups regarding the schools. The speakers bureau can be expanded to include topics beyond the school itself. For example, a teacher might be a "rockhound," or the custodian might be a classical music "bug." Invite them to be listed as available speakers for classes and community groups.

246 **Form Business Partnerships.** Establish business partnerships with local fast food restaurants and allied businesses. Establishments such as McDonald's, Burger King, Pizza Hut, Dairy Queen, and other companies are willing to explore the potential of having certificates made up for free food for certain tasks accomplished. Food chains and local food outlets are happy to get young people into their businesses. School-business partnerships send a positive message to the community.

247 **Perform For Senior Citizens.** Teach students to square dance, then have them go out and perform for senior citizens at a nursing home or retirement community. The students will never encounter a more appreciative audience. They will learn a special skill while serving the community.

248 **Join A Service Club.** Educators who join and participate in community organization meetings such as Rotary, Chamber of Commerce, YMCA, Lions, religious groups or other organizations related to community life make a major contribution to community outreach. The best way to have good public relations is to be a positive and visible force in the community.

249 **Create A Slide Show.** Put together a slide show about local schools. Make it generic in nature so that it can be used at an open house, a kindergarten orientation, a civic club presentation, as a continuous showing at parent-teacher conference time, or any other place where it may be appropriate.

250 **Contact The Media.** Contact the local radio or television stations, talk with the news manager, and suggest that a program about schools would be attractive to viewers and listeners. Arrange for student volunteers to serve as hosts. Point out upcoming school activities, special honors, new programs, and the many fine activities that take place in schools.

251 **Support The Community.** Arrange for student organizations to participate in special community projects. For example, Adopt-A-Highway projects, disaster relief drives, clean-up days, and senior citizen functions all help students become community-minded and enhance the image of the school.

252 **Maintain A Wake-Up Call.** Local radio DJ's will be happy to make wake-up calls for students each morning. This will give the radio stations the opportunity to get "on the band-wagon" of encouraging students to attend school.

253 **Invite Leaders For Lunch.** Invite key community leaders for lunch. Be sure to include a get-acquainted time and a time for explaining the school program. Make sure new community leaders are included.

254 **Form Community Organizations.** Hold special luncheons or dinners prepared by home economics classes for various community organizations. The Rotary Club, Lions Club, Chamber of Commerce, and Board of Realtors are some of the organizations that might accept.

255 **Practice Community Sharing.** Each class selects a local business or organization, such as a hospital or senior citizens' home, and shares a particular homemade gift or song. This says "thank you" to the community.

256 Involve Senior Citizens. Many senior citizens are looking for ways to be of service. If a new student is having a difficult time, invite a senior citizen to do a project with the young person during the school day. With proper supervision both are likely to profit.

257 Give A Hand. Encourage the entire school family to reach out to feed the less fortunate for the holidays. This school effort can be done in cooperation with the police, fire department, or other community organizations.

258 Display Student Work. Student work is often seen within the school, but what about placing student work in banks, real estate offices, airports, libraries, grocery stores, and wherever citizens gather? It is a good way to say "We are proud of our students," to invite positive self-concepts in students, and to create good school/community relations.

259 Organize A Book Collection. Encourage all classes to organize and conduct a mass drive for books and magazines to be donated and delivered to the homeless shelters or other human services for individuals and families in need.

260 Celebrate American Education Week. Invite the community to an open house to visit the school, tour the building, observe demonstrations, and see the classrooms during school hours.

261 Welcome All New Families. The important thing here is to send welcome notes whether or not the family has children. They may have children in time; even if they don't, help them to feel that they are part of the school family.

262 Adopt-A-Class. Businesses "adopt" a class. In doing this they will receive art work for their seasonal store windows and an open invitation to visit the school. They also receive personal invitations and free tickets to school events.

COMPUTERS

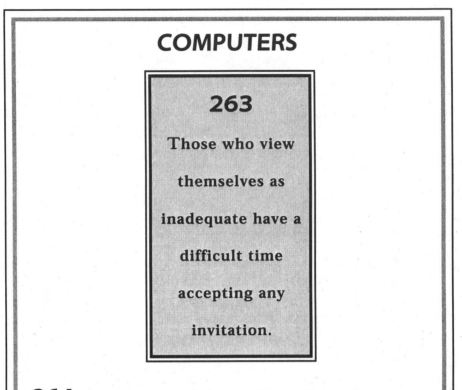

263

Those who view themselves as inadequate have a difficult time accepting any invitation.

264 Place Computers In The Library. Computers can be placed in the library for students to use to write papers for class or other assignments. There are also some fascinating programs that can be purchased for the computer that provide information and games in academic areas such as math, language arts, and business.

265 Provide Opportunities For Success. Some students who have disabilities that prevent them from writing clearly thrive on computers. Using the computer allows them great opportunities to express ideas.

266 Create Computer Stations For Teachers. Create opportunities for teachers to easily access computers, perhaps by creating a special computer station for them. Many teachers appreciate the opportunity to use computers to prepare materials for class and for professional activities. It also helps to provide classes for teachers who would like to learn to use computers.

COUNSELING SERVICES

> ## 267
>
> A caring
>
> disability is when
>
> no one cares
>
> enough to invite.

268 Post College Offerings. Keep up-to-date on classes taught at neighboring colleges and universities. By posting these offerings, counselors invite students and fellow professionals to take advantage of these opportunities. Better still, organize a carpool for attending them.

269 Hold A Happy Hour. Open up the counseling center occasionally after school for teachers and others to enjoy refreshments and conversation. If space is limited, go to a larger room. This hour can be an excellent opportunity for the staff to develop a feeling of community as well as a time to present a mini-session of new ideas. These gatherings may be for relaxing, with no business, or they may combine pleasure with some professionally interesting idea.

270 Encourage Participation. Invite faculty members to visit the counseling center to help decide about guidance and counseling programs and activities to be used in the school. Also solicit suggestions from parents, students, and teachers about ways that the school counseling program can be improved. The suggestions and participation of all present will add to their feeling that this is "our" program. Equally important, these contributions will strengthen the program.

271 Offer Refreshments. Receiving visitors to the counseling center is like having company at home. Keep the coffee brewing and tea bag ready. Have a snack or treat available, no matter how humble the fare. Sharing food and drink is among the most ancient symbols of community and helps to provide a friendly atmosphere.

272 Brighten Up The Center. Hang posters and get some living green plants. Make the counseling center office a place where people want to come. Have comfortable furniture for both students and adults—and no thrones facing undersized chairs!

273 Invest A Penny. "A penny for your thoughts." Tape a brand new penny to a small card and send one to each teacher in the school. On the card ask each teacher for suggestions about how the counseling center can be of special assistance to him or her.

274 Hold A Sharing Session. Plan and conduct a "drop-by" session in the counseling center where folks can enjoy refreshments and be involved in a brief training program on such topics as stress reduction, contract grading systems, or other innovative offerings. It need not take long for some quality sharing.

275 Organize A Crisis Team. Organize a trauma or crisis team to help faculty, staff, and students deal with death, divorce, drinking, drugs, or other painful and often unexpected circumstances.

276 Conduct Group Guidance Activities. Whether in the regular classroom or with the counselor, these are special times to address topics of interest and to develop understanding among students. Feature special activities for new students.

277 Create Registration Packets. Counselors may find it helpful to provide students and parents with a registration packet that includes information on testing, graduation requirements, and available student services. This is in addition to the student handbook or information packet used to familiarize faculty, students, and parents with counseling services available.

278 Include The Leadership. Principals, supervisors, school board members, and others appreciate being invited to the counseling center for activities and events. Such events build personal relationships among counselors and other professionals. They also provide counselors with the opportunity to show the value of the counseling program.

279 Strangle The Paper Monster. Unfortunately, counselors are sometimes among those who create forms for teachers and students to fill out. Keep the methods of communication between counselors, fellow professionals, students, and families as easy and simple as possible. Time is precious. It should be valued highly and not spent on relatively unimportant requests.

280 Serve The Family. Make regular contact with families to let them know the activities and programs provided by the counseling program. Counselors can offer programs on helping students through a divorce, enriching relationships, dealing with death, working with home discipline, and the like.

281 Practicing Counseling Skills. An inviting counseling center looks like someone:

smiling	sending a friendly note
being relaxed	sharing an experience
listening carefully	giving wait-time
opening a door	yielding interest
sharing laughter	learning names
being on time	being polite

COURTYARDS

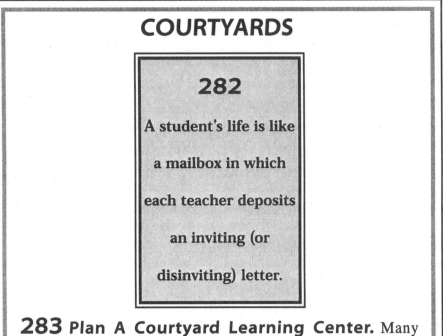

282

A student's life is like
a mailbox in which
each teacher deposits
an inviting (or
disinviting) letter.

283 Plan A Courtyard Learning Center. Many schools have courtyards. These areas offer a great opportunity to contribute to the learning and living environment of a school. Senior students might have the privilege of having their lunch there, and classes might utilize it for instructional purposes. A courtyard with a brick patio, benches, picnic tables, trees, perennials, bird feeders and bird houses can do wonders for a school. Students, parent volunteers and community contributors can transform any courtyard.

CREATIVITY

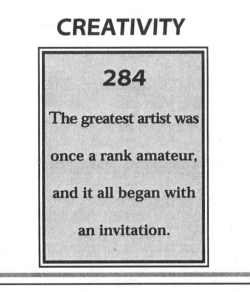

284

The greatest artist was
once a rank amateur,
and it all began with
an invitation.

285 **Take Time For Creative Thinking.** Devote seven minutes a day to creative thinking. Once a day ask students to let their imaginations run free. Ask how many different uses they can think of for red bricks, or have them consider absolutely every way to make school more enjoyable. No holds are barred, and there are no right or wrong answers. It is easier to tame a wild idea than to spice up a dull one.

286 **Build A Poem.** Writing a sixteen-line poem can seem like an impossible task for some students. To avoid the problem, ask each student to write a one-line poem on an agreed-upon topic (a sunset is an excellent subject). Collect the one-line poems and select a small group of students to put the lines into a poem. The result is usually outstanding.

287 **Invent Games.** Divide the class into teams and ask them to invent a game that the world has never seen. Each team invents a game, gives it a name, and then teaches it to the class.

288 **Encourage Topsy-Turvy Thinking.** Great discoveries are the result of recognizing what others have seen but have not grasped. Encourage students to put things together so that they make a new kind of sense. For example, what if everyone had twenty fingers, or one finger? What if the earth were shaped like an egg? The possibilities are limitless.

289 **Attack Boredom.** Take a few risks to improve life in classrooms. For example, devise puzzles, exercises, visual demonstrations, role-plays, competitions, and challenges. Boredom is the number one enemy of classroom learning.

290 **Get Those Creative Juices Flowing.** Encourage students to think creatively by using such statements or questions as:
- What inventions are needed that have not yet been invented?
- In one paragraph, write an outline for a creative story for children.
- Design a better way to read a newspaper.
- Create an advertising slogan for life and death.

These are just the beginning of being creative.

291 **Check "Peeves."** Everyone has special pet peeves—things that bother or annoy them. Ask students to write down several pet peeves. (The teacher writes them down too.) Then, ask students to write creative suggestions about how these peeves might be successfully addressed or eliminated.

292 **Choose An Honor.** Ask students what honor they would most like to receive:

       A. Medal of Freedom: Dedicated to the highest standards of achievement.

       B. Medal of Honor: Gallantry above and beyond the call of duty.

       C. Olympic Decathelon: Win ten events in Olympic games.

       D. Honored Artist at Lincoln Center: First achievement in drama, music. Have them talk about their choices and the reason for making them.

CULTURAL DIVERSITY

293

The best

invitation is to

communicate that

we are BOTH

able, valuable,

and responsible.

294 Celebrate Black History Month. Hold a special assembly to commemorate this important time. During February, bulletin boards, displays, morning announcements, essay contests, and assemblies depict the school's recognition of this event.

295 Honor Diversity. Students and teachers may represent different regions, lifestyles, and ethnic origins. This diversity presents a rich opportunity for students, teachers, and staff to learn the customs, traditions, and heritage of others. Students learn to understand other students better and enjoy sharing experiences and perceptions. Diversity can be celebrated by special meals, festivals, assemblies, storytelling hours, and visits to classrooms by foreign exchange students.

296 Celebrate Other Cultures. Chinese, Mexican, Hawaiian, West Indian, African, Italian, and German are only some of the many cultures whose food can be saluted with the school menu. With a little planning, the menu can highlight Heritage Day, cultural activities, or a social science unit.

297 Hold A Cultural Heritage Assembly. Provide a yearly special assembly program to celebrate cultural diversity. This could include a concert of African music, a special speaker on cultural heritage, or brief skits on the importance of understanding and appreciation of cultural differences.

298 Share The Glory. Create and support a school policy that class officers, school cheerleaders, and students selected for responsibilities should be drawn from as many student groups as possible. Creating an "out" group is a sure way to elicit student hostility and misbehavior.

299 Be Cautious With Generalizations. Try to relate to people, not labels. Take time to know students as individuals, not as groups. Generalizations deny students their dignity as unique human beings. This is particularly true when it comes to sexism, racism, and other forms of prejudice.

300 **Appoint A Cultural Teacher.** Ask students to assume the role of "teacher" and present a program about their cultures. For example, a farm child might present a program on farming or even invite the class for a tour of the farm. An Asian student might explain the Chinese New Year and follow it up with some oriental food. The opportunities are many.

301 **Treat People As Individuals.** A threatening danger in education is to lump people into groups and see them in generalities. ("You know how they are.") It is important to remember that each person is an individual, and that each is unique.

DEMOCRATIC VALUES

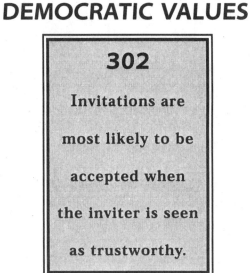

302

Invitations are

most likely to be

accepted when

the inviter is seen

as trustworthy.

303 **Seek Faculty Consensus.** Seek and value opinions from all the faculty and staff and be open to alternative viewpoints. A useful technique is to hold a monthly brainstorming session with faculty and staff to look at concerns and possible solutions.

304 **Offer Ideas For Consideration.** Practicing the democratic ideal, which presents options, shows that the school believes people are able, valuable, and responsible. For example, "Have you considered?" or "What else might you have tried?" reflects faith in people and in their self-directing powers. It also is an invitation to others to use these powers.

305 Hold Informal "Buzz" Meetings. An informal "buzz" meeting within the classroom invites everyone to express his or her feelings in a nonthreatening environment. Set some basic democratic ground rules and a time frame, and then listen. Sharing perceptions develops understanding and relationships.

306 Promote Democratic Values. Holding mock elections, trials, debates, and role-plays, developing class constitutions, and organizing team-building projects are all excellent ways to encourage democratic values. These can be topped off at the high school level by holding voter registration drives for seniors.

307 Follow That Bill. Involve students in following a particular legislative bill as it works its way through the legislature. Normally, legislators are happy to get involved in this democratic process. Should the opportunity present itself, testifying at a hearing is a learning experience that is unforgettable.

308 Involve Students In Decisions. Where possible, involve the entire school family in the decision-making process. Students can participate in such areas as rules of conduct, academic expectations, activities, even textbook reviews and teacher selection. The main point is to make it OUR school, where WE have some influence on what happens to US.

309 Plan Regular Classroom Meetings. Involve students in some classroom decisions by holding weekly class meetings. These may provide excellent opportunities to discuss rules, express feelings, and introduce new students to a nonthreatening environment.

310 Display Emblems Of Trust. Sometimes educators are so concerned about the prevention of vandalism or thievery that schools become like prisons, with locks on everything and warning signs everywhere. The result is that vandals and thieves appear to be running the school, creating distrust in everyone. When chances of success are good, educators should treat students as trustworthy. Students will live up, or down, to expectations.

311 **Work Together On Policies.** In developing policies to govern student behavior, it is important to include as many staff members as possible. Systems of management for hallways, classrooms, entrances, the cafeteria, and the like can best be developed through collaboration with custodians, food-service workers, counselors, the principal, and other professionals. No teacher or classroom is an island. Policies require support from everyone in the school.

DIFFICULT SITUATIONS

312

Because some

invitations are

rejected does not

mean all will be.

313 **Be A Scuba Diver.** Some authorities encourage teachers to take "a deep breath" to reduce tension. A better way is suggested by scuba divers who are taught to exhale all bad air before inhaling. The next time a child is getting on one's nerves, slowly exhale the stale air from lungs, and follow this with a gradual deep breath. It reduces tensions immediately.

314 **Climb Mad Mountain.** When individuals come to an educator with anger, in reality they are climbing "Mad Mountain." The wise educator lets them climb the mountain without interruption. When the angry person reaches the top of mad mountain, the anger will cool and he or she will start down the other side. It is then that the educator can offer condolences or explanations. Let the angry person climb the mountain. If not, he or she will start at the bottom of the mountain again with twice the momentum.

315 **Cool Down First.** Avoid responding while angry or upset. It is important to let tempers cool down a little before taking action, particularly when something is being put in writing. It is difficult to justify disinviting behavior even if the behavior is understandable.

316 **Keep Things Simple.** When someone comes with a complaint, stay on that complaint. Try not to multiply the problem with counter-complaints or angry exchanges. Sometimes "second-level" problems become greater than the original ones. Listen carefully and be willing to express regret. (This is not an apology.) Where possible, take some action. Complaints are not always negative; some can be tremendously valuable.

317 **Read Behavior Backwards.** Rather than looking only at the behavior of a misbehaving student, an angry parent, or a cranky colleague, consider how the person might be viewing self, others, and the world. Sometimes students see themselves as more disinvited than undisciplined. By looking at the "why" of behavior, it is much easier to understand the "what."

318 **Rehearse The Future.** Often educators who make errors in judgments go over their errors again and again in their minds. In effect they practice their mistakes: "How could I have been so stupid?" A better way is to ask "How will I handle such situations better next time?" Only by thinking of positive future responses can reviewing past errors be beneficial.

319 **Reprimand In Private.** Respecting students' need for privacy when the need to reprimand arises is very important. Students behave quite differently when they know they are being observed by peers.

320 **Make A Wish.** In working to improve a student's behavior call that student aside and give three positive comments regarding his or her work, then quickly follow it up with your "wish." For example, "Mary I am pleased with your work, and I like your enthusiasm and leadership. I wish that you would get to class on time. Will you do this?" This is a very mild-mannered way of encouraging desirable student behavior.

321 Pay Attention To The Ice. The fox in Aesop's fable avoided falling through the ice on the pond by listening to its sound. Successful teachers sense the mood of the class and avoid discipline problems before they happen by such means as moving towards the source of misbehavior, lowering one's voice, or shifting to a more interesting part of the lesson.

322 Practice The Language Of Opportunity. The cup is not half empty; it is half full! Practice using words that encourage positive approaches to situations. For example, change the word:

"Visitor"	to	"Guest"
"Problem"	to	"Opportunity"
"Lost"	to	"Misplaced"
"Can't"	to	"Won't"
"Motivate"	to	"Invite"
"Must"	to	"Prefer"
"Always"	to	"Sometimes"
"Never"	to	"Seldom"

Words do influence thoughts.

323 Say No Slowly. When it is necessary to give a negative response to a request, at least let it come after having listened carefully and fully to the request. One of the worst indictments that can be leveled against educators is for someone to say: "They wouldn't even listen to me!" The failure to hear the person out can hurt more than the negative answer. Invite each person to fully express his or her request before it is accepted or rejected.

324 Show Respect. When an angry parent or visitor enters the school, ask the secretary in the guest's presence to hold telephone calls until the conference is over. This is an important way to let the agitated guest feel important.

325 **Soften The Blow.** When everything has been done to avoid student failure, and yet the student continues to fail, positive procedures should be developed to inform parents as early as possible of possible failure. Information should be given to them regarding summer school, counseling services, and tutoring arrangements that are available through the school.

326 **Practice Active Listening.** Listening carefully is an important way that educators can help to minimize feelings of hostility on the part of parents, students, or others in the community. By listening, the educator is showing clear respect while gaining an understanding of the situation.

327 **Provide Help.** In situations of serious injury or illness of a school family member, marshal support in the form of expressions of concern and love. Help can also be very tangible, such as blood drives, food collections, or monetary assistance through fund collections.

328 **Learn To Relax.** Relaxation techniques are vital for teachers and students. Ask everyone in class to sit erect in their chairs, exhale slowly, then take a slow deep breath. The surge of oxygen will help to relieve tension and clear thought processes.

329 **Eat Crow With Style.** Even perfectionists will make mistakes, so when mistakes happen, remember to:
- Analyze the mistake and think how to keep it from happening again.
- Listen to those who complain about the mistake and accept their feelings. (Acceptance is not agreement.)
- Once the mistake is corrected, never refer to it again.
- Use mistakes as important lessons for the future.

DISCIPLINE (CLASSROOM)

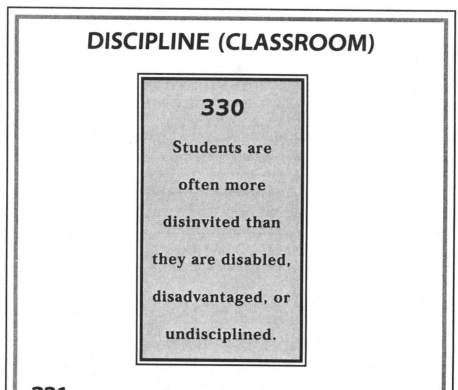

330

Students are

often more

disinvited than

they are disabled,

disadvantaged, or

undisciplined.

331 Invite Explicitly. The more explicit an invitation, the more likely it will be accepted. Vagueness leaves others wondering, "What is meant by that?" For example, saying, "Let's go to dinner on Thursday evening at 7:00" has a much better chance of being accepted than "Let's get together sometime." Be clear with what is expected of students.

332 Look For Causes Of Misbehavior. It is important to work on causes of discipline problems in schools; the causes are not always people. Often the system is at fault. For example, running in the halls may be caused by minimal time periods between classes. Changing the system sometimes eliminates the problem.

333 Lower The Volume. Often educators will raise their voices when classroom discipline begins to break down. Practice lowering your voice when you want someone's attention. The surprise works almost every time. Make a commitment to speak more softly.

334 Give Positive Directions. Too often directions are negative. For example: "Don't talk," "Stop running," "Quit that." Try making directions positive by focusing on what should be done, rather than what should not be done: "Please walk," "Please be still."

335 Stretch Muscles. If students are fidgety or restless, it is a good idea to take a minute for stretch exercises. Ask everyone to stand and do a few simple exercises.

336 Disperse Energy. A military rule is to never place bombs, gasoline, and highly combustible materials in one location. Spread the challenging students around the classroom or school.

337 Relate To People. Be cautious in substituting the label for the person. For example, a person might be exhibiting very disinviting behavior, but this does not mean that the person is a disinviting person. Sometimes labels can be worse than the problem itself.

338 Reconceptualize The Situation. Often concerns appear unsolvable because they are viewed from only one vantage point. Changing conceptions can change situations. For example, a student with a high energy level can be a problem, but he or she can also be a valuable source of assistance to the teacher.

339 Cheat The Devil. The old adage that the "Devil has work for idle hands" seems to hold a suggestion for good discipline: Keep students busy. Giving all students clear responsibilities via a job chart (collecting material, arranging the classroom, tidying up, working together on assignments). Keep students busy and involved. Lessons should be, as much as possible, activity based. These require a lot of teacher preparation but they pay off in good discipline.

340 **Maintain An "Opportunity Center."** Rather than relying on the traditional "In-School Suspension Center," change the name (and concept) so that it is proactive rather than reactive. The "Opportunity Center" should be counselor-oriented and give the student the opportunity to atone for mistakes and make plans to avoid them in the future.

341 **Arrange A "Down-Time" Corner.** In the lower grades an overstuffed armchair, an old sofa, a rocking chair, or even an old bathtub piled with pillows, along with a rug, books, and a game or two can be just the thing to help a student overcome anxieties or anger stemming from some temporary crisis in his or her life.

342 **Practice The Five C's.** Try to resolve any troublesome situation at the lowest possible "C":

> **Concern:** The situation requires attention.
> **Confer:** Explain the concern to the student.
> **Consult:** Caution the student regarding penalties.
> **Confront:** Give a serious warning of the possible penalty.
> **Combat:** Administer a reasonable and enforceable penalty.

343 **Use The No-Cut Contract.** Explain to students the long-lasting effects of racist, sexist, or other negative comments. Make a "no-cut contract" in writing with students. Everyone agrees that in this classroom:

> "I will not put you down."
> "I will not put myself down."
> "You will not put me down."
> "You will not put yourself down."

If a student or teacher breaks the contract, he or she should be gently but firmly reminded of the agreement.

344 Keep It Simple, Sweetheart (KISS). Educators who propose a large number of school rules are ensuring that rules will be broken. The fewer the rules, the fewer chances there are to break them. A few good rules in the best interests of everyone can be agreed on by students and faculty.

345 Practice Never, Never. Never leave a classroom unattended (the professional is legally and ethically responsible for the welfare of students in his or her care), never compromise discipline (nothing positive will occur if a classroom or school management system is not in effect), and never confuse students about the schoolwide discipline policy (insure that students understand what is expected of them).

346 Use The Ol "Switcheroo." When younger students come up and offer a report about another student, politely interrupt and say, "Oh, I can tell you are about to say something very good about your friend." They may say "yes" and continue the discussion, or decide not to say any more.

347 Keep The Milk From Spilling. There's usually not much difference between effective and ineffective educators after the misbehavior has occurred. The secret is to keep the volcano from erupting. By keeping eyes and ears open and sensing when difficulties are approaching, preventive strategies can be applied and little problems can be handled before they become big ones.

348 Ask For The Order. When educators ask explicitly and clearly for what they want, there is a likelihood that they will get what they ask for. Vagueness creates misunderstanding, so invite explicitly. For example, "John, I want you to open your book and read page 30" is much more effective than "John, settle down." Be specific on how students can improve behaviors.

349 **Focus On Behavior.** Keep the topic of conversation on action. For example, the question, "Why did you trip Charlie?" will lead to all sorts of time-wasting, creative comments. A better question is "What did you do?" After attempting evasion, most students will admit to the undesirable activity. Once the behavior is admitted, the stage is set for the development of more socially appropriate behaviors.

350 **Play Low Cards First.** When a player in a card game has to decide which card to play, he or she most often wants to take a trick "as cheaply as possible." It makes little sense to play an ace when a lower card would win just as well. Similarly, a teacher wants to invite good discipline with as little energy and time expended as possible. Working ""smart" is more important than working "hard."

351 **Check The Timing.** Few things are more important in good discipline than timing. Too much or too little, too soon or too late, can weaken the best intention. So ask: "What invitation to good behavior is most likely to be accepted by this student at this moment?" Choosing the right moment for the right move is a hallmark of good discipline.

352 **Catch Them Being Good.** Are students behaving especially well today? Try saying: "Class, I'm really pleased that you all worked so hard on your math exercises. Thank you for making my job pleasant!" This small investment of time could result in multiple dividends in the classroom climate.

353 **Talk Things Out.** Dialogue is an essential and telling activity for human beings, so try to talk things out. Find how things seem from the student's point of view. Wherever possible, deal with a misbehaving student privately, on a one-on-one basis. An informal chat might keep a volcano from erupting.

354 **Make The Unacceptable Acceptable.** When a student has acted in an unacceptable way, say: "I think you can behave better than this." Point out the correct way of behaving: "Talk quietly, so you won't disturb others," then say: "This is the way I want you to behave." This encourages clear communication and student responsibility.

355 **Identify The Difference.** There is a vast difference between "rejection" and "nonacceptance." That a student has not accepted the teacher's request does not mean that the student has rejected it. Sometimes a little patience and time can make all the difference. The world was not created in a day, and neither is good student discipline.

356 **Hold Your Point!** Champion bird dogs are judged in part by how long they "hold the point" when they detect a covey of birds. Similarly, champion teachers are judged by the way they consistently and dependably invite good discipline. Creating positive classroom discipline is a marathon, not a sprint.

357 **Set Rules Together.** Work with students to decide upon some general classroom rules and penalties for infractions. It's harder for students to argue with self-imposed rules of conduct.

358 **Sink The Hook.** When requesting appropriate behavior from a student, form the habit of saying: "Will you do this for me?" When the student answers in the affirmative, then the student has given his or her word. This is a powerful determinant of future behavior.

359 **Keep A Balance.** It is a good idea to keep enough money in the bank to cover the checks written. The same is true in the classroom. Be sure that the consequences described for certain behaviors are reasonable and can be carried out. Write only checks that can be cashed.

360 Present Real Options. To give options that are totally out of balance ("You can stop talking or you can go to the principal's office") is playing with a stacked deck. Offer choices that demonstrate that you respect the student and that communicate a desire for the student to learn from this discipline situation. A teacher can ask the student for options as consequences for disruptive behavior. A disruptive student may have the choice of going to a time-out area, the counselor's office, or staying after school to help the teacher.

361 Use Common Sense. This means that threats are never made that can't be carried out, and that if behavior is considered unacceptable one day it is unacceptable on other days. Nothing will take the place of common sense in maintaining good discipline.

362 Skin Your Own Alligator. Classroom discipline is primarily the responsibility of the classroom teacher. The teacher should seek outside assistance (i.e., sending students to the office) only when it is really needed and when the teacher cannot handle the situation.

363 Establish A Routine. Have a systematic routine for all classroom procedures. By creating and maintaining an established way of administering classroom routine (distributing materials, preparing the audiovisual, collecting assignments), classroom discipline is improved and time is used effectively.

DISCIPLINE (SCHOOLWIDE)

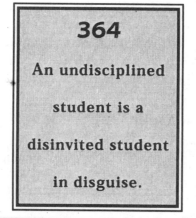

364

An undisciplined

student is a

disinvited student

in disguise.

365 **Capture The Cheese.** A "big cut" out of a yardstick is placed in the cafeteria. Each inch on the yardstick represents one day of school. A laminated picture of a piece of cheese hangs at a predetermined point on the yardstick (a goal of twenty-three days out of forty-six days, for example) and a laminated picture of a mouse will hang on the far left. At the end of each day, if no referrals have been made for misbehavior on the bus, on the playground, in the hallways, or in the cafeteria, the principal will announce that the mouse will move one inch closer to the cheese. If a referral has been made, the mouse stays still. If the mouse reaches the cheese before the end of the grading period, a schoolwide reward is earned by all classes (FREE RECESS). If the mouse gets the cheese three out of the four grading periods, a picnic is held on the next to the last day of the school for everyone.

366 **Give B.U.G. (Being Unusually Good) Awards.** During a grading period, all teachers and staff are given thirty B.U.G.s to distribute to students who are "being unusually good" (behaving appropriately) in the hallways, cafeteria, and playground. Teachers may not award B.U.G.s to their own students. When students are awarded a B.U.G. they can color it, print their name on it, and display it on their classroom bulletin board. The class receiving the highest number of B.U.G.s at the end of set period receives a special B.U.G.

367 **Understand Fads.** Students are constantly moving in and out of fads (dress, hair style, idols, language). While educators may not agree with these fads, it is important to recognize that they exist. As long as these fads do not violate school policies or public law, they can often be tolerated until they lose popularity and go away of their own accord.

368 **Create A Place For Everything.** To avoid confusion and poor control situations, require that everything in the classroom has its proper place and is kept there. This avoids loss of time looking for one thing or another.

DISPLAYS

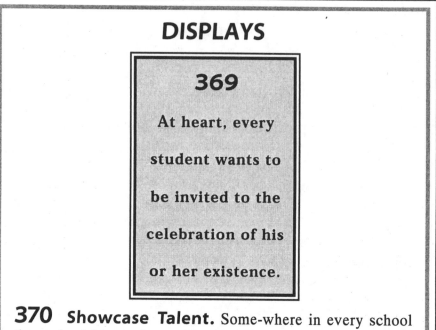

369

At heart, every
student wants to
be invited to the
celebration of his
or her existence.

370 Showcase Talent. Some-where in every school there should be at least one showcase to display art work, collections, trophies, academic awards, and special projects. Showcases are intended to handle items that will not fit on a bulletin board. Showcases can be mounted on a wall or can be movable. Use safety glass in the case.

371 Obtain a Foyer Showcase. A display case can be placed in the entranceway to show examples of student work in various academic disciplines. It can be changed every other week.

ECOLOGY

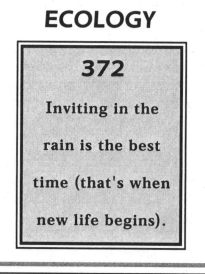

372

Inviting in the
rain is the best
time (that's when
new life begins).

373 Join The Green Team. Recycling is a national commitment. Encourage an ongoing composting, returning, and recycling program at the school, with recycling bins for glass, cans, newspaper, and copying paper.

374 Adopt-A-Highway. The entire school family can adopt a length of highway to keep clean of litter. The litter (cans, glass, paper, etc.) can often be recycled at a school recycling center.

375 Clean Up A Creek. Too often brooks, streams, and creeks are littered with trash and debris. The school can sponsor a clean-up-the-creek on a Saturday and accomplish a good deed for Mother Nature.

376 Honor Nature. Establishing a classroom or school greenhouse, or planting and cultivating a garden plot is an excellent way to teach students that food does not come from the supermarket. It is also an excellent way to teach earth science.

ENTRANCE

377

A series of

disinvites makes

being invisible

very inviting.

378 Smell Good. An automatic air freshener, mounted over the entrances of the school, can do wonders for a school. Faculty, staff, students, and visitors will be highly impressed with how well the school smells.

379 Establish An Information Booth. For large secondary schools, a full-time aide monitors traffic, provides added security, and gives direction and assistance to all visitors.

EVALUATION: STUDENTS

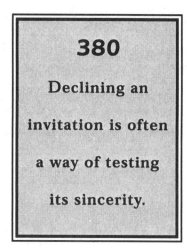

380

Declining an

invitation is often

a way of testing

its sincerity.

381 Give Prompt Feedback. Information on performance, when long delayed, loses much of its educational value. This is particularly true of younger students. Make a rule that student work will be evaluated and returned as quickly as possible.

382 Encourage Student Self-Evaluation. When pupils complete independent study units, extra credit assignments, or any special projects, consider the use of student self-evaluation. Questions like, "What do you like about your work?" or "If you were to do this project again, what would you change?" encourage a valuable personal critique.

383 Practice Spin Control. When students receive poor progress report cards, personal contact should be made with those students to discuss methods of improvement. If the situation seems very dim, a parent conference should be set up. Don't wait for the parent to take the initiative. The school should request the conference.

384 Bypass The Test. As an incentive for good effort, give pretests to determine how much students already know about a subject. Those who pass the "pre-test" are able to bypass the test itself. Those who are excused from taking the test can spend time practicing other skills.

385 Offer Multiple-Choice Comments. On "objective" tests, such as multiple-choice, fill in the blank, true or false, leave room following each item for the student to make comments regarding his or her answer. Sometimes the answer is perfectly acceptable when the teacher understands the *context* in which the answer is given.

386 Add Spice To Tests. Give student a choice of questions to answer on tests. For example, part of the test might state: "Write a question that you wish were on the test and answer it." This gives students the chance to highlight some aspect of the course they enjoyed and studied. Open book tests can help in developing overall comprehension skills. Whatever the format, remember two basic rules of testing: (1) Give frequent tests on small amounts of information, and (2) evaluate student work promptly.

387 Use Any Color But Red. Traditional red, black, or blue notations on student papers will not get the attention that a vibrant new color will achieve. Switch to magic marker, a highlighter, or any color other than red. The color red has negative connotations, particularly in China where it is considered to be the color of death!

388 Raise-A-Grade. Students who bring up at least one grade without dropping any other grade are listed on the "Most Improved Student" roster. They might also have their names placed in a drawing for several prizes to be given each grading period. Even a 65 percent "success" for a student whose usual grade is 60 percent is worth recognizing. ("Raise your average five points and you become a member of the Plus Five Club.") It is vital to recognize effort and reward improvement.

389 Accent The Positive. If a student has a score of 90 percent on a twenty-word spelling test, the student has either gotten "two wrong" or "eighteen right." Fractional equivalents, for example 9/10, 17/23, are more beneficial than -1 or -6. Check all the *correct* answers on work sheets and focus on what the student did well. Students learn more from success than they do from failure.

390 Handle The Unacceptable. When a student hands in something unacceptable, try this statement: "I think you can do better than this." Point out ways for improvement, encourage student efforts, and ask the student to try again. If an assignment is totally incorrect, state: "Please see me so we can go over this together." Then be sure to follow through with the student.

391 Add Report Card Commentary. Written comments on report cards are highly beneficial to both students and parents. Make brief written comments on every report card. Grades become important because of the comments the teacher took time to write.

EVALUATION: TEACHERS

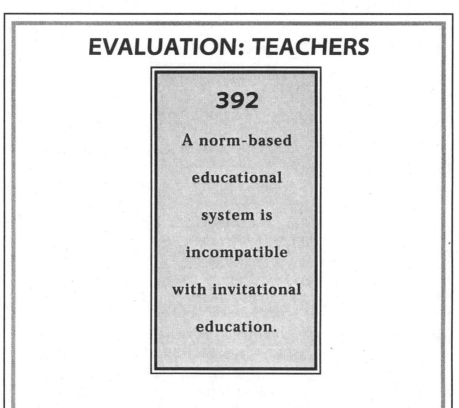

392

A norm-based

educational

system is

incompatible

with invitational

education.

393 Ask For Parent Feedback. Prepare conference evaluation forms for each parent-teacher conference for *parents* to complete. This may provide valuable suggestions for future conferences.

394 Enrich Teacher Evaluations. When the principal is planning to observe and evaluate a teacher, it is important to meet with the teacher first and find out what the teacher plans to do. Looking at behavior only, and not at intentions as well, leaves out half the picture.

395 Seek Feedback From Students. At the end of each semester seek suggestions from students. Find out how they evaluate the educative process and what could be done to make it better. This shows respect for the opinions of students while strengthening the teaching/learning process.

FACULTY LOUNGE

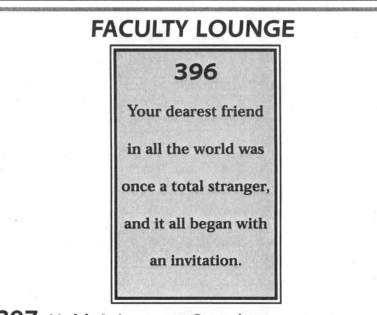

396

Your dearest friend

in all the world was

once a total stranger,

and it all began with

an invitation.

397 **Hold A Lounge Opening.** Work with parent groups and the school social committee to make over the faculty lounge. Area rugs, fresh paint, clean windows, living plants, a coffee machine, a professional library shelf, a microwave, nice lighting, and comfortable furniture can work wonders (and don't overlook the washrooms). When the lounge is freshly decorated, arrange for refreshments and send an invitation to all faculty to attend the "grand opening." They will love it.

FACULTY WORKROOM

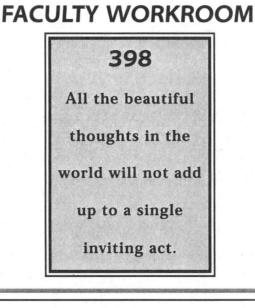

398

All the beautiful

thoughts in the

world will not add

up to a single

inviting act.

399 **Keep The Place In Shape.** Sometimes when it is everyone's responsibility it becomes nobody's responsibility. To insure clean, orderly, and attractive workrooms and lounges, arrange a sign-up sheet for everyone to take one week as workroom or faculty lounge monitor.

400 **Ease Up On The Xerox.** Encourage faculty and staff to make a special effort to reduce the amount of copying done for worksheets. Having students write the same material on the blackboard while other students copy the material accomplishes the same thing with more learning for everyone. (To further save paper, be sure that a step-by-step instruction manual is available for all machine operations.)

FAIRS

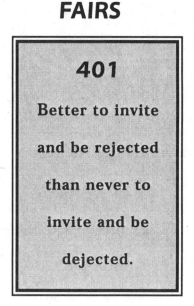

401

Better to invite

and be rejected

than never to

invite and be

dejected.

402 **Have An Academic Fair.** Having some type of *academic fair* each year, where student projects are displayed, will lead to an improved curriculum. Academic fairs can include a P. E. demonstration, an art fair, a social studies fair, a math fair, or any other curriculum area. Build the fair around an open house with hallways designated as Math Hall, Language Arts Hall, and Art Hall, and involve parents in the project. Prizes may be given. Certificates should be given to every student who has a project. The enthusiasm toward the subject area will increase considerably with parents, students, and teachers.

403 Hold A Book Fair. Holding an evening book fair, where used books are donated for purchases at the fair, can generate funds for the school while encouraging reading for everyone. To encourage attendance, the book fair can be combined with a chili dinner or ice cream social. Left over books can be contributed to charities.

404 Create An International Fair. An international fair can be held where as many nationalities as possible are spotlighted. The fair can include displays, dances, costumes, and other ways to teach appreciation for diversity and to welcome all nationalities to the school.

405 Celebrate Grandparents' Day. Early in September is Grandparents' Day in the United States. However, many schools find it advantageous to have a special Grandparents' Day around Thanksgiving, Hanukkah, Christmas, Easter, or Passover. Special projects and inviting ways of treating grandparents when they come to school, such as musical programs, refreshments, and lunch or activity passes, add to good public relations.

FAMILY OUTREACH

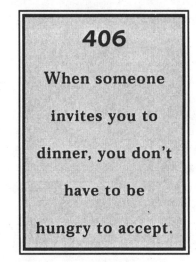

406

When someone invites you to dinner, you don't have to be hungry to accept.

407 Send Positive Notes. ("Caught you being good.") During the first grading period, each teacher writes and sends home one positive note until every child has received a note. Try to identify areas of strength and send notes home early to avert possible concerns.

408 Search For Strengths. Instead of seeing only the negative in a student's family, look for resources or strengths. Develop an attitude based on encouraging families to use these strengths to work for the best interests of their child. This attitude can be expressed in the teacher's lounge, at meetings, and with the child and family. And remember to use "single parent family"—*never* "broken home."

409 Go First Class. Take pride in every letter or announcement that goes home from the school. Check carefully for spelling, syntax, and grammar. Every communication that goes out from the school represents the school and everyone in it. Correspondence to families should not be written in haste or anger.

410 Communicate Positively. Too often the majority of messages sent home are essentially negative: "Bill forgot his gym socks," "Lucy was late again." To avoid emphasizing the negative, make a vow that *most* personal notes going home will be *positive*: "Bill is making great progress in rope-climbing," "Lucy has written some beautiful poems." In a student's life every success counts.

411 Make Hospital Visits. One special caring act is for members of the school family to visit any student who is in the hospital. Stop in to say hello, give the student a book, and wish him or her a speedy recovery. These few minutes will brighten a child's day and are greatly appreciated by the family. The effects of this visit will be long-lasting. The secret is to make sure that teachers let everyone know when students are in the hospital.

412 Work For Parity. Some families have little money for such things as field trips, laboratory fees, or extra-curricular activity fees. Students whose families cannot afford fees are at a real disadvantage. Establishing special funds, grants, or fee waivers for such students is essential. Often community partnerships can help with this situation by donating items or providing money for grants or fee waivers.

413 Protect The Single-Parent Child. Sometimes father-son breakfasts, or mother-daughter lunches can be discriminating against single-parent or parentless children. To guard against this, ask students engaged in making gifts for Mother's Day or Father's Day to "make a card or gift for someone who is very important in your life." This gives a sense of belonging and purpose to children who only have one parent, if that.

414 Schedule Convenient Conferences. Try to schedule these important parent-teacher meetings at a time convenient to parents (early morning or late afternoon) and be on time. Choose the most comfortable place available to meet and offer parents a comfortable place to sit. A little privacy is also appreciated.

415 Address The Singular. It is preferable to address form letters to "Dear Parent" rather than "Dear Parents." Many students come from single-parent families, and using the collective form of greeting could be disinviting.

416 Look Beyond The Surface. Some children may appear less attractive than others. Their clothing and behavior may encourage one to focus his or her attention on other more appealing students who appear to have more potential. Teachers who expect less of these children communicate a strong message to parents. Looking beyond the surface, a teacher can find potential in every student.

417 Begin In A Positive Way. Begin each conference with an informal positive comment about the student. During the conference avoid educational jargon, be a good listener, and be as optimistic as possible. After the meeting, a follow-up note to the parents is appreciated. Inform the student that the teacher enjoyed meeting and talking with his or her parents.

418 Plan An Ice Cream Social. One way to increase parent participation at open houses is to have an old-fashioned ice cream social in the school dining room or at an outdoor area. Convince the PTA or parent council to provide all the ingredients, including ice cream and toppings plus volunteers to run this social. Even hard-to-reach parents are likely to show up for an ice cream social.

419 Learn Names Of Parents. It is useful to determine the correct names of parents. The parents of some children have remarried and their names may differ from the child's. For example, John Johnson's mother may be named Mrs. Garcia after her second marriage. Use the correct name, and pronounce it correctly.

420 Celebrate The Family Night. Students, families, and community members are invited to observe student demonstrations in gymnastics, see the computer lab in operation, visit the art and music rooms, and view exhibits. Add games, activities, and movies to make the family night enjoyable for everyone.

421 Break Bread With Parents. Invite parents to a breakfast, brunch, or lunch in the school dining room. Have faculty and staff present to greet the parents. Students can design name tags for their parents. For variety, the school could feature a "Parent Coffee/Tea," a "Doughnuts with Caregivers," a "Meet My Older Friend" or even an old-fashioned picnic on the school grounds.

422 **Maintain Open Communication.** Keep parents up-to-date concerning school activities and student progress by sending home newsletters, notes, or school newspapers. It is helpful for parents to know about student and staff achievements, upcoming school events, and school plans for new programs or projects.

423 **Search For Family Talent.** Design a survey that fits the needs of the school and send it home to parents. Make sure that the survey is well written with specific goals in mind. Parents filling out these surveys are also asked to sign up to be on a speakers bureau for the school. Parents can provide talent for school variety shows, class presentations and demonstrations, and all sorts of hobbies and crafts.

424 **Form A Parent Advisory Council.** Establish a parent advisory council for parent involvement in the school. Not only will it be a wonderful "sounding board" for the principal and faculty, but the council's involvement in the school is invaluable. The additional activities and opportunities it provides for students is amazing. Request advisory council input on further improvement of the school.

425 **Involve Parents.** Ask parents for suggestions about class speakers, homework assignments, special programs, and school functioning. Parents can be asked to participate in school decisions even if they are not on an official school commitee.

426 **Ask "How Are We Doing?"** Prepare and distribute to parents an annual evaluation form ("parent report card") to help the school evaluate various school matters. Parent comments and concerns will help build a better school. Be sure to listen carefully to what parents report and also to what is implied but not said.

427 **Be Aware Of Family Difficulties.** It helps to learn about any family difficulties or changes that might influence a child's behavior or performance in school. A death or divorce in a family may affect a child's concentration or attention in class. Teachers who know these things are likely to be more understanding and supportive of the student.

428 **Organize Parent Support Groups.** Many families are facing special challenges, and organizing a parent support group can be of great help to parents. The groups can be facilitated by a school counselor. Groups such as "Single Parents," "Parent-Student Relations," "Parents of Special Students," "Step- or Blended Family Experience," or "Parents of Substance Abusing Teens" can be organized.

429 **Create Parent Study Groups.** Take time to plan and hold parent/student workshops on such topics as choosing a college, drug and alcohol abuse, parenting skills, sex education, conflict management, and academic achievement. Many parents are looking for an opportunity to become involved in the school program. Counselors are the school's primary resource for these activities.

430 **Involve Family Members Judiciously.** Because families are very busy and members have little time to spend with each other, it is important when assigning homework that requires family participation to insure that it is meaningful. Projects that involve family members need to be given thoughtfully and judiciously.

431 **Design A Home Communication Sheet.** The school can design a Home Communication Sheet with three columns. The first column has student's *name*, second column has *positive note home*, third column has *call home*. Have the secretary type in all the names or have the computer generate a student list for each classroom. Give them to the teachers and ask them to keep track of their communications with parents. This check sheet is in addition to regular parent/teacher conferences.

432 Communicate Positively. Too often messages sent home are negative and turn parents away from the school. Send home far more positive notes than negative notes. Inform parents specifically what they can do to help their child and what school resources are available to them. Invite parents to visit the school and see the academic program firsthand.

433 Celebrate Grandparents. Hold a "Grandparents' Day" when grandparents are invited to come to school and enjoy refreshments and student performances and activities. For those students without grandparents, check with retirement homes about an "Adopt A Grandparent Program."

434 Eat Doughnuts With Dad. Each student brings his or her dad (or special male friend or relative) to school before class for doughnuts and coffee, milk, or juice. Often the doughnuts will be donated by local merchants. During this doughnut time, organize a "men's team" or "Security Dad" program for the school.

435 Form "The Men's Team." Establish a fathers' (or other special adult male relative or friend) club to promote involvement of adult males in the school. These men provide critical role models for young boys with or without fathers at home.

FEEDER SCHOOLS

436

After the verb "to love," "to invite" is the most beautiful verb in the world.

437 Feed The Feeders. Send copies of honor rolls, student awards, bulletins, newsletters, and other information to feeder schools. This lets the feeder schools know that their major contributions to student success are appeciated. Former teachers get a thrill out of learning how well their "old" students are doing at their new school.

438 Visit Feeder Schools. Arrange for faculty and staff to visit feeder schools as often as possible. These visits promote curriculum articulation, make transferring students feel more comfortable, and give opportunities for teachers and staff to become familiar with each other and with the different school environments

FIELD TRIPS

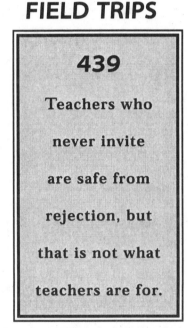

439

Teachers who

never invite

are safe from

rejection, but

that is not what

teachers are for.

440 Use Field Studies. An excellent way to encourage academic achievement is to get students out of the classroom and reinforce material already covered in the classroom course content. For example, visiting a graveyard can encourage writing and stimulate imagination. Ask students to select one stone and answer: "What was this person like? What took place in society during this period of the person's life?" Advanced students can even conduct actual research on the person in library files and old newspapers.

441 Express Thanks. When students are taken on field trips to visit museums, parks, or exhibits, it is important that teachers and students collectively or individually write thank-you notes to the hosts. This reinforces good manners, shows respect for others, and builds good school-community relations.

442 Appoint Field Generals. Involve students in the planning of field trips. Have them become responsible for student behavior, logistics, meals, and the like. When the field trip is completed, encourage the "generals" to share their experiences with other classes.

HALLWAYS

443

The greatest

barriers to

inviting are

self-imposed.

444 Mount Hallway Mirrors. Obtain full-length shatterproof mirrors and place several around the school where students, faculty, and staff can see themselves as they pass by. This invites neatness and a sense of good grooming. Place a sign at the top of the mirror that says: "PROUD MEMBERS OF THE BEST SCHOOL IN _____(name the state)."

445 **Obtain Some Carpet Runners.** Even the hardest working rubber mat can't handle the moisture from wet shoes on a rainy day. Eventually the hallway floors near the outdoors become slippery. To avoid this, ask some local floor covering companies if they will donate a 6 × 20 foot carpet runner for the main lobby.

HANDBOOKS

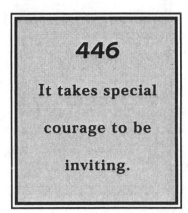

446

It takes special

courage to be

inviting.

447 **Develop A School-Family Handbook.** Prepare a handbook of things students, parents, faculty and staff should know about their school. This information includes policies, directions, where to seek assistance, and other pertinent information that everyone needs to know. Distribute handbooks at the beginning of each school year.

448 **Create An Interview Handbook.** Develop a handbook for high school students that describes how to write resumes and interview for a job. The handbook provides descriptions of how to conduct oneself during an interview. It offers sample questions of what interviewers might ask of the student, and what the student might ask the interviewer. Model resumes might also be included in the handbook.

HOLIDAYS

449

You are always

invited when you

are giving the

party.

450 Remember The Holidays. Holidays are sprinkled throughout the school year. They offer special ways to invite creatively. Halloween, Thanksgiving, Christmas, Hanukkah, and Passover are only a few of the many special events that can be celebrated with special foods, decorations, and themes.

451 Promote Holiday Poetry Writing. Encourage students to write poetry that expresses their feelings and ideas concerning various holidays. The poems can be printed in the school's newsletter and posted on bulletin boards throughout the school and in the community. Some students may be encouraged to send their poems to local or state publications.

452 Guess The Halloween Whoooo. Invite students to write brief descriptions of themselves without giving their names and place these descriptions in a box. (They could be attached to pictures or cutouts of ghosts, witches, or pumpkins.) Each student draws a description, reads it aloud, and everyone tries to guess who the description fits.

453 Use The Pumpkin. Around Halloween, a pumpkin can be a great teaching aid. It can be used to talk about the importance of farming and transportation, and about the process of growth and reproduction. Make a pumpkin pie, save and plant the seeds, and the class has the bonus of a jack-o'-lantern.

454 Practice Christmas Sharing. In place of a gift exchange among children at Christmas, have children *earn* money that they will give to a needy family, a charitable group, or organization. Let students decide where their money will go. The school can also serve as a collection agency for food drives during the holiday season.

455 Invite Some Resolutions. Happy New Year! Now's the time to invite students to write a "New Year's Resolution." Ask them to describe some positive changes they wish for themselves. Seal the resolutions in a special container and location and have the children open them later in the school year.

456 Save Holiday Cards. Save the more beautiful pictures and messages written on holiday cards. These pictures and messages can be cut out and used as note pads for all occasions.

457 Plan A Christmas Surprise. At Christmas, unknown to the pupils, the classroom teacher provides little giftwrapped prizes for various tasks. The surprises may be given for neat desks, super monitors, and most improved, most helpful, and most cheerful students. Make sure that each student earns one gift.

458 Buy Half-Price Greeting Cards. Christmas, Halloween, Hanukkah, Valentine's Day, Easter, and other holiday cards always go on sale immediately after the holiday is over. This is a very smart time to buy cards for next year's mailing to students, colleagues, and friends.

HOMELESS

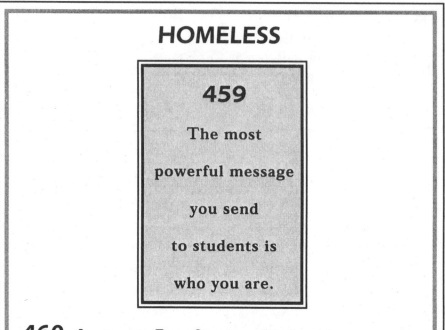

459

The most

powerful message

you send

to students is

who you are.

460 Arrange For Access. Work with community health care services to provide health training and service access for homeless families. Even hospitals can sometimes offer personnel to help homeless families in basic health care and preventative measures. It might also be possible to locate retired medical personnel (nurses, doctors, dentists) who would volunteer their services to help the homeless.

461 Visit The Shelters. Arrange for some professional from the school to visit each homeless shelter in the area to encourage parents to enroll their children in the school. At this time it is important to demonstrate honest care and to show parents how they can have access to various school programs.

462 Say Hello, Goodbye, Hello. Children of homeless families may suddenly appear at school at any time of the year, and may just as suddenly disappear. This is because homeless families are usually seeking work or better living conditions. After disappearing for a while, the same children may reappear. It is hard on the bookkeeping, but it is critical to greet the child warmly and welcome the child back again and again.

463 Arrange Transit. Sometimes homeless students have a hard time getting to and from school, not to mention finding a way to participate in after-school activities. Negotiate a special pass with the local transit authorities, or seek grants or business support to develop a transportation arrangement for homeless students.

HOMEROOMS

464

People want to

be affirmed in

their present

value while being

invited to realize

their potential.

465 Arrange Happy Homerooms. Start off each week on a positive note by asking students in homerooms to tell one happy thing that happened either to themselves personally, or to someone else in the community. Each student is given the opportunity to contribute his or her views, and each contribution is important.

HOMEWORK

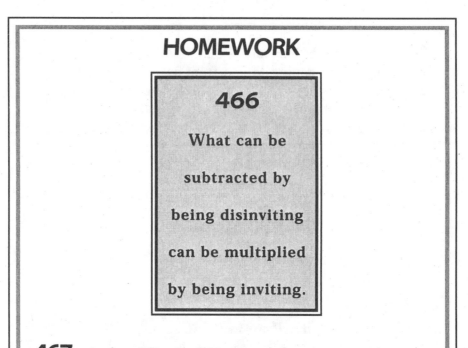

466

What can be

subtracted by

being disinviting

can be multiplied

by being inviting.

467 **Assign "Can-Do" Homework.** Homework should be assigned so that each student has an excellent chance of success. To assign homework when there is reason to believe that some students cannot do it is simply causing trouble. Assign homework that students *know* they can do. When they ask, "Why such homework?" the answer is: "Practice, practice, practice is the key to *retention* of learning.

468 **Be A Bulldog.** It is critical to let students know that the teacher will not give up on them. For example, when a student does not turn in a homework assignment, the persistent teacher says, "This assignment is important. When will you get it in?" It is not a matter of *if*, but *when*. The student has clear responsibilities. The assignment may be late, but it must come in.

469 **Organize A Homework Hotline.** Obtain volunteers to staff a homework hotline to help students resolve difficult problems. The volunteers do not provide answers, but help the student work through the questions. If funds permit, it is great to have the hotline staffed by fully certified teachers with expertise in discipline areas.

ICE BREAKERS

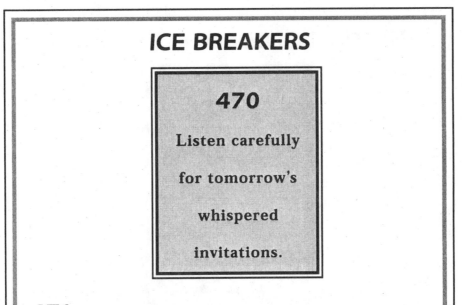

470

Listen carefully

for tomorrow's

whispered

invitations.

471 Guess "Who I Am." Ask students to write on index cards some biographical information (that does not invade confidentiality) that explains who they are but does not make it too obvious. For example, students may list hobbies, trips taken, talents, unusual interests, and other unusual items. Collect the cards, distribute them randomly, and ask everyone to find the secret person.

472 Select The Most Important Object. Ask students to select one thing they brought to school that day that is most important to them. In other words, if they had to give away everything they brought to school but one thing, what would that one thing be? And then ask them to tell why it is so important to them.

473 Find The Most Appealing Thing. The goal of this ice-breaker is to look around the classroom and to find the thing that is the most appealing to a student. It may be the bulletin board or the video monitor or the window. Ask each student to write down on a piece of paper which object he or she finds most appealing. Then after all students have picked an object ask each student what is appealing about that object. For example, a student might pick the globe in the room because of the desire to travel or a fascination with people who live in other countries.

INVITING ONESELF PERSONALLY

474

Think of the

nicest invitation

you could send to

others and send

it to yourself.

475 Treat Yourself. Make a pledge to do something special for yourself in the immediate future. Treat yourself to a shopping trip, a new outfit, some quality down-time, a good book, a favorite meal, a play, a movie, or other enjoyable event.

476 Be A Good M.D. Over 85 percent of all the medical attention an educator receives is self-delivered. Each of us places bandaids on cuts and scratches, prescribes medicine (aspirin, vitamins, pills), removes splinters, massages stiff muscles—the list is endless. Healthy educators work at being good M.D.s to themselves by taking responsibility for their own well-being.

477 Build A Personal Fort Knox. Start a special file of letters, awards, notes, gifts, and other recognitions you have received over the years. When you begin to feel down or "burned out," visit your own personal Fort Knox and restore your spirits, renew your faith in your own ability, and help yourself to help others.

478 Renew A Friendship. Call or write an old friend you have not talked with in a long time. Perhaps you can work out a date for a dinner, concert, movie, or other special event.

479 **Practice Positive Self-Talk.** Negative self-statements, such as "I could never do that," can discourage one from perceiving oneself as able, valuable, and capable. Change negative self-talk to positive self-talk:

"I could never do that."	to	"It may be hard, but I'll do it."
"I never do anything right."	to	"It is only human to make mistakes."
"I can't..."	to	"I will try..."
"I'm hopeless..."	to	"I have difficulty with this, but I will keep trying."
"No one could like me..."	to	"There are people who will like me for myself."
"I should not have said it."	to	"It would have been better if I had not said it."

480 **Plan An Adventure.** Visit travel agencies and load up on travel brochures. Dream a little. You will be tomorrow where your ideas of today take you.

481 **Brag A Little.** Teachers are quick to post their students' achievements, but seldom do they mention their own successes. Share accomplishments with students. A nice letter, a prize won, or a photograph of a new car or patio can cause students to celebrate too.

482 **Defuse Your Self-Talk.** Often when faced with a difficult day or situation, one's feelings can seem overwhelming. One way to reduce feelings of stress and anxiety is to examine one's self-talk. Self-statements which heighten one's anxiety and stress include:

"This is going to be a terrible day." (mind-reading);
"I never do anything right." (all-or-none reasoning);
"It's always my fault." (personalization);
"No one thinks I'm a good teacher."(overgeneralization);
"I should have known better."(should thinking);
"I am responsible for this." (control thinking fallacies).

483 Practice Cognitive Clarity. When one identifies distortions in thinking which heighten anxiety and stress, it is useful to defuse these distortions by practicing "cognitive clarity."
- Examine the evidence that supports your assumption. (Is it *always* your fault?)
- Throw out absolutes. (*No one* thinks you are a good teacher?)
- Take responsibility for what you can do. (Are you really responsible for this situation?)
- Dump the idea that a person can be perfect. View mistakes as opportunities for learning.

484 Explore A Library. For a relaxing and enjoyable experience, spend a few hours browsing in a library. Wander through stacks in subject areas that you don't usually visit. You will have an exciting world of knowledge at your fingertips, and it costs nothing.

485 Take A Trip Down Memory Lane. One way to become more sensitive to students is to try to remember what school was like when you were in a particular grade. These questions might jog your memory:
1. What was your teacher like?
2. Who were your friends in the class?
3. What do you remember most about the class? Invites? Disinvites?
4. How did you behave in class?

486 Find Down-Time. Take time to relax and get your mind off professional matters. A book or movie, a change of scenery, gardening, tennis, long walks, a hobby, a nice nap, a bike ride, a pot of tea, making homemade soup, buying a carnation, and visiting a flea market, used bookstore, or local travel agency, can all help to refresh yourself.

487 Live With A Flourish. Find satisfaction from many sources, such as a hobby or activity unrelated to your professional life. As much as possible, surround yourself with things you like. Laugh a little. Take a few risks, try something new, travel, and assert yourself. The goal is to avoid drabness.

488 Take Pleasure In Being Alone. While too much isolation can be bad, time to be alone, to enjoy stillness, to contemplate and meditate on who you are, where you came from, and where you're going, can be both personally and professionally rewarding. The goal is to be at one with the world and with the spirit.

489 Give Yourself A Gift. Make a pledge to do something special for yourself, and only for yourself, in the immediate future. Give yourself a hot bath, a window-shopping trip, a new outfit, a special hour for coffee, a good book, a special meal. When you celebrate yourself, it's easier to celebrate others.

490 Become A Photographer. If you don't already have a reasonably good camera, buy one and start a new hobby. There are few things more enjoyable (to many of us) than walking down a forest trail or other natural area and taking photos of the many wonders you'll be sure to encounter.

491 Leave School At School. This is easier said than done. There are always papers to grade or report cards to complete. Try to manage your school time so as to whittle away those chores at school. The daily frustrations that accompany any career which involves interaction with others should remain behind school doors. Instead, enjoy family, friends, and freedom.

492 Take A Few Risks. When chances of success are good, it usually pays to take a few chances. Accept new people, ideas, and experiences. Show your feelings and share your humanness—be willing to express care and affection.

493 **Sharpen The Image.** It's almost never too late to improve on one's appearance. Losing weight, getting a lift, dyeing hair, having teeth straightened (or whitened) all add to positive self-esteem.

494 **Adopt Two Cats.** If your home seems a little lonely, head for the SPCA and adopt two neutered cats. Their curiosity with each other and with you will offer a lot of companionship. Be sure that you're willing to make the commitment of ten to fifteen years, the average cat's lifetime.

495 **Talk With A Friend.** Talk things over with a colleague whom you consider to have good sense. Just talking about concerns helps to avoid a lot of guilt and anxiety.

496 **Attack The Clothes Closet.** Go through the clothes closet and give to charity everything you have not worn in three years. Get rid of everything you don't like.

497 **Get A Jump-Start.** Here are two dozen examples of the many good ways to recharge your batteries:

Visit a museum	Get active in politics
Join a book club	Attend church or synagogue
Start a hobby	Bake some bread
Try a new recipe	Take a nap
Go shopping	Brew some tea
Buy new clothes	Throw a party
Learn a new skill	Take a hike
Take music lessons	Talk with a friend
Get a massage	Play golf
Go fishing	Attend a play
Take some photographs	Call a friend
Write a relative	Take a bubble bath

498 **Be A Good Manager.** Make it a rule that you will delegate every classroom chore that can be delegated to students or parent volunteers. This includes collecting and distributing materials, arranging the classroom, and placing things on the blackboard. Good teachers are good managers.

INVITING OTHERS PERSONALLY

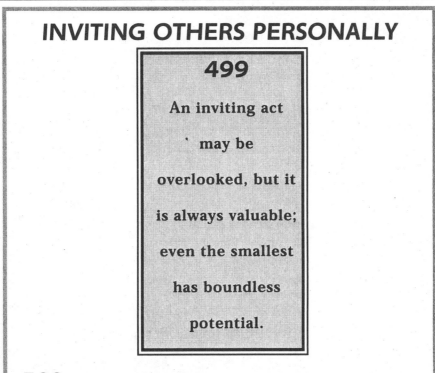

499

An inviting act

may be

overlooked, but it

is always valuable;

even the smallest

has boundless

potential.

500 Throw A Party. Invite friends and colleagues over for an informal get-together. And don't forget the neighbors. The way to have friends is to be one.

501 Greet Others. Make the effort to say "hello" to as many people as possible when walking down the hallway. Greeting students and others in the hallway and expecting a proper response costs nothing and builds good relationships.

502 Get To Know Others. Get to know colleagues on a somewhat personal level. Learn the names of their family members or close friends and periodically ask about them. Remember all of us have a life outside the school.

503 Share Your Person. Let the students know that you have many dimensions other than just teacher. Share anecdotes about your family or pets. Let students know your feelings about books or movies, even share your moods. You will be surprised at how thoughtful and caring students can be when you tell them you have a headache.

504 Share With Friends. Keep friends in mind when you receive materials in the mail or read about books or activities relating to their interests. For example, if a friend collects cat figurines, pass on any information about interesting cats. Share magazines, news clips, and brochures that may interest your friends. To care is to act caringly, and almost anything can be used to let your friends know you care.

505 Practice Happy Talk. Try to start every class with some good news about what is happening in the classroom, school community and the world. Five minutes of "happy talk" can set the stage for a super class period.

LANDSCAPING

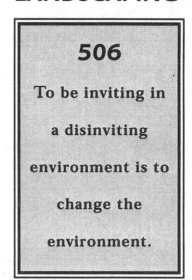

506

To be inviting in

a disinviting

environment is to

change the

environment.

507 Add That Special Touch. The addition of such simple items as a split rail fence, a few picnic tables, some benches, a flower garden, some shrubbery, a bird-bath or bird feeders can do wonders to make the landscape of a school more comfortable, appealing, and attractive. Perhaps the PTA can provide the funds for these improvements.

508 **Organize A Neighborhood Cleanup Day.**
Pick a Saturday in the spring for a special neighborhood cleanup. People who live close to a school sometimes complain about students cutting across lawns and throwing paper around. Spending a Saturday improving the community landscape can be a great way to promote friendship with the school's close neighbors.

509 **Use Tree Power.** Few things can beautify a landscape as much as a tree. The school science club can celebrate Earth Day by planting trees. The entire school can plant trees and name them to commemorate people or events. Fully-grown trees can be "adopted" by a class to insure that they receive proper care.

510 **Plant Flowers.** A most inviting sight is to arrive at a school and see flowers blooming. This planting effort can be made into a learning experience as well, in biology, science, civics, or art. Each class might agree to create and maintain a flower bed.

511 **Hold A Saturday Planting Party.** Ask everyone in the school to spend some time on a Saturday morning to help improve the appearance of the school with plants. Parents, students, and others can bring bedding plants. Even nurseries may donate a plant or two. School service clubs and garden clubs can also be invited to participate and join the party. Serve refreshments to everyone.

512 **Lay Out A Trail.** Where space and conditions permit, a nature trail or jogging path on the school grounds can be both educational and healthful. Science clubs can add markers to the nature trail, and students and adults can use the trail for jogging, walking, and talking about concerns.

LESSON PLANNING

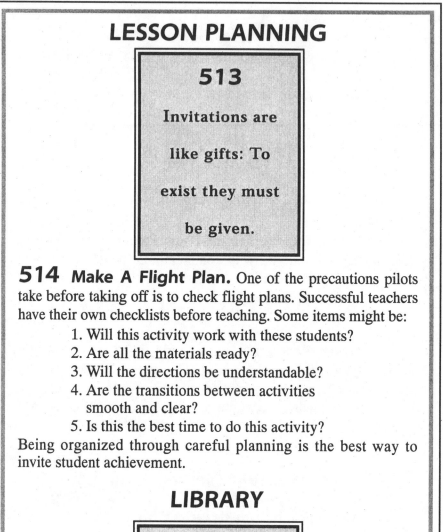

513

Invitations are

like gifts: To

exist they must

be given.

514 Make A Flight Plan. One of the precautions pilots take before taking off is to check flight plans. Successful teachers have their own checklists before teaching. Some items might be:

1. Will this activity work with these students?
2. Are all the materials ready?
3. Will the directions be understandable?
4. Are the transitions between activities smooth and clear?
5. Is this the best time to do this activity?

Being organized through careful planning is the best way to invite student achievement.

LIBRARY

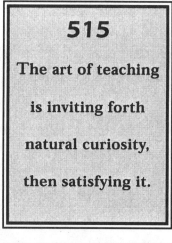

515

The art of teaching

is inviting forth

natural curiosity,

then satisfying it.

516 Give Books Away. It is always advantageous for the librarian to have some paperback books to give away as gifts or special recognition for students. Arrange to have a good collection of books at a variety of reading levels.

517 Keep A Brag Book. Keep an album in the library of all current newspaper articles involving students, teachers, staff, and alumni. The "Brag Book" should include all activities and honors that take place during the school year. At the end of the academic year the Brag Book can then be placed in the school archives.

518 Encourage Bibliotherapy. Arrange a special area in the school library for books which address current teen problems. Be sure to include books on health issues, interpersonal relations, conflict resolution, and what it's like to be "the new kid on the block."

519 Let Students Evaluate Materials. Invite students to critically evaluate reading material. *Listen* to the children. Often, what adults think is appealing is not appealing to children. Making recommendations about reading materials invites a feeling of importance in students.

520 Identify A Character. Take pictures of book characters and have them duplicated on paper for 4-inch badges. Each staff member wears a book character. When a student can identify who the character is and something about the character, the student gets the badge. Students will spend time in the library trying to find unfamiliar characters.

521 Provide Book Marks. Make available strips of stiff paper so that students can make book marks for themselves and each other with decorations, good wishes, and quotes on them. This helps to prevent the earmarking of book pages.

522 Hold A Used Book Sale. Once a year ask everyone in the school family to contribute books for a book sale. This encourages reading while raising money for library projects.

523 **Get Everyone A Library Card.** Plan a class field trip to the local public library so students can see what the library has to offer. During the visit invite each student to apply for a library card.

LOBBY

524 **Brighten The Lobby.** First impressions are all important, so pay special attention to the school's entrance way. Comfortable benches for guests, a welcome sign, living green plants, student work on attractive bulletin boards, and, most importantly, cleanliness all contribute to the school's hospitality. Where conditions permit, open doors to the school are a special welcome.

LOST AND FOUND ARTICLES

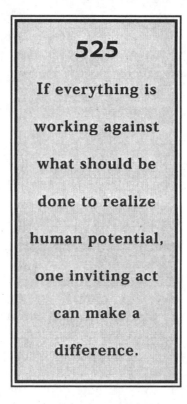

525

If everything is

working against

what should be

done to realize

human potential,

one inviting act

can make a

difference.

526 Post Lost And Found Signs. It is important to post signs explaining where to go in the school in case an item is lost or found. In elementary and middle schools, a "Lost & Found Box" works well. Students and parents can check there first for lost items. Valuable items such as money or watches can be held in the principal's office. At the end of each semester, all items can be placed on display for students (and parents) to examine and identify. Unclaimed articles are always welcomed by community relief organizations.

MEETINGS

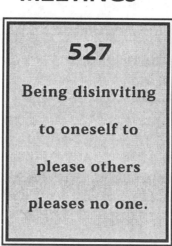

527

Being disinviting

to oneself to

please others

pleases no one.

528 Create Positive Meeting Agendas. Begin each meeting with a report of all the honest success experiences that have taken place since the last meeting. Keep reports brief (see "Time Management") and to the point. Provide participants with the time to share their ideas. In even the worst of situations there is always room for optimism, so share efforts, accomplishments, and success stories.

529 Encourage Participation. To obtain more participation at meetings, discussion on important issues can be facilitated by dividing and subdividing the group. Start with pairs, then with groups of four, then groups of eight. It is difficult to remain silent when a participant is fifty percent of the group.

530 Invite The Editor. Newspaper editors can usually provide a most interesting meeting. They can talk about public opinion and how to get the news out about the good things that are happening in schools.

531 Alternate Meeting Times. Meetings are most often held on "tired time" (after school). Try scheduling an early morning breakfast meeting. In return for a few dollars and a few hours planning, a delicious breakfast can be prepared at school.

532 Keep Meetings On Time. Everyone can make a vow that all faculty meetings will start on time, end on time, and will never go over one hour. One simple technique to enforce the rule is for everyone to stand at the fifty-five minute mark and continue standing until the end of the meeting. It probably will not go over an hour!

533 Encourage Attendance. Improve attendance at meetings by making them enjoyable. Door prizes can be given, or a dollar bill can be taped under some lucky person's chair. A fun activity, such as a drawing, a contest, a sing-along, and refreshments can keep things alive.

534 Float The Meeting. Most school meetings are held in the same place, such as a library, conference room, or cafeteria. To add spice and variety to meetings, hold them in different locations. Select a classroom or gym, and ask the teachers or coaches to serve as hosts. It takes a few minutes to organize tables, chairs, and other setups, but it is well worth the time and effort to obtain a fresh perspective.

535 Plan Comfortable Meetings. A careful check of facilities before an activity begins insures that personal needs are considered. This includes refreshments, seating, lighting, temperature, materials, restroom facilities, and related items of comfort. Meetings go best when participants feel cared about.

536 **Use One-Minute Ice-Breakers.** To warm up any meeting, ask participants to take one minute to do something like: (1) Share what is found in one's pocket, (2) Describe the best book one ever read, (3) tell the most terrible pun, or (4) share the most trivial trivia. These little one-minute activities can get a meeting off to a good start.

537 **Make The Participants Comfortable.** A stretch is always welcome if the participants have been seated for some time. (And they work to make the presenter comfortable too.)

538 **Get People Involved.** From the beginning make sure it is "our" program. Organize subcommittees for publicity, refreshments, greetings, registration, name tags (with first names in BIG LETTERS), decorations, and other tasks. Give subcommittees responsibilities, as opposed to jobs, and encourage them to contribute ideas.

539 **Start Early.** It takes months to build enthusiasm and attendance, so begin early! Reserve facilities, contact speakers, organize subcommittees, and arrange other services you will need. Choose a meeting place that will add to the program.

540 **Make Careful Plans.** Once the purpose, theme, and presenters for the program have been identified, write letters of confirmation to the presenters which state date, day, year, location, time, theme, and financial arrangement.

541 **Prepare For Publicity.** Obtain a photograph, vita, and presentation abstract from your speaker. These will be needed to prepare news releases and brochures.

542 **Be Creative.** Cash in on a special season, date, event, holiday, or other happening. For example, one school system used a presidential nominating convention theme for an opening in-service. Each school was a "delegation." During a roll call of states (schools), each principal announced the number of his or her "delegates," and described the glories of his or her school.

543 Delegate Everything. Delegate all responsibilities to subcommittees. The program committee should be free to insure that subcommittees are functioning properly and to fill any last-minute gaps that occur.

544 Invite Everybody. There is value in inviting secretaries, custodians, bus drivers, teacher aides, school board members, school nurses, local parent groups, and student representatives. Taxpayers can be invited through the local paper. Even if the invitation is not accepted, good community relationships have been cultivated.

545 Arrange Video And Audiotapes. Ask speakers for permission to video or audiotape their talks. Make sure taping is done by experts. A bad tape can be worse than no tape at all.

546 Beat The Publicity Drums. Send news releases to all local newspapers, television and radio stations, and education newsletters. Make announcements at all professional meetings, on all bulletin boards, and in at least one U.S. postal mailing.

547 Explain The Merits. Publicity should include who is presenting, what will be the benefits of attending, when and where the meeting will be held, and why people should want to attend this program.

548 Contact Neighbors. Send an invitation to neighboring school systems, private schools, colleges, universities, and others and suggest that they send representatives to your meeting. They may want to return the courtesy one day.

549 Assist The Speaker. Let the speaker know the approximate number of people you expect to attend, their roles, interests, and concerns. Information on local "color" and topical information is appreciated by speakers.

550 **Call The Police.** Inform the local police of your meeting and request that officers be assigned to assist participants in and out of parking lots before and after the meeting.

551 **Notify Restaurants.** Call nearby restaurants and alert them that they may have a large number of diners on the meeting day. Also, a list of local restaurants with their locations will be useful.

552 **Book A Photographer.** Ask a volunteer photographer to record the day's activities. These photos will be useful in unexpected ways, such as follow-up publicity and future newsletters.

553 **Check Restrooms.** Are there sufficient facilities, particularly if participants are mostly of one sex? Print signs that convert the names of some restrooms.

554 **Hang Welcome Signs.** The first thing your participants should see are large "Welcome" signs. Additional signs can give directions regarding parking, location of meeting rooms, refreshments, and restrooms.

555 **Roll Out The Red Carpet.** Arrange accommodations for your speakers at attractive locations and send your speaker a guaranteed confirmation. If there are unique products made in your area, the speaker may enjoy purchasing something to take home.

556 **Check The Temperature.** Air conditioners may need to be turned on, or windows opened, the night before. Heating units may need to be started early. Ask technicians to be available during the program in case the meeting area gets too hot or too cold.

557 **Out-Fox Murphy.** Remember Murphy's Law: "If anything can go wrong, it will." Double check all reservations and commitments. A successful meeting belongs to everyone. The meeting that fails belongs to the program committee.

558 Break Bread Together. As participants arrive for the meeting, station greeters at the doors who point the way to doughnuts, coffee, tea, and juice. Providing simple fare reflects friendship and respect.

559 Squeeze People Together. It is better to have a few people left standing than to have several hundred participants in a 2,000 seat auditorium. If a large auditorium must be used, rope off the back sections and hang "wet paint" or "reserved for the choir" signs on the ropes. To ask people to "please move forward" is a *poor* way to start a meeting.

560 Test The Microphone. An ineffective microphone can defeat the best speaker. Have it checked several times. To be safe, ask an audio professional to stand by with an alternate system in case of problems.

561 Strike Up The Band. As participants arrive, arrange "live" music to establish a mood for the meeting. Music may be provided by a pianist, a choir, a teachers' group of musicians or singers, or whatever. If all else fails, use a record player and play favorite records.

562 Start On Time. Do not punish the people who arrive on time for the benefit of those who come late. If the program starts on time, a dependable policy for future meetings is being established.

563 Keep The Agenda Light. Avoid the common error of too much program. Resist last-minute requests for announcements or program additions. The best speaker will fail if she or he must follow a long, drawn-out program.

564 Make The Speaker Visible. Participants *see* a speech as well as hear it. Brighten the lectern area and make sure the speaker is elevated enough to be seen clearly.

565 Provide Talk-Time. Participants like to talk as well as listen. Where possible, build in small group activities. If this is not possible, consider "buzz groups" in the general meeting, where people are asked to turn and "buzz" with their "neighbors" for several minutes.

566 Expedite The Invoices. As soon as resources permit, mail travel and honorarium checks to all presenters. Also pay refreshment and accommodation bills quickly.

567 Prepare For The Next Time. After the program, send a note of thanks to everyone who contributed to the program. Also, hold a follow-up meeting with chairpersons to debrief the program and think of ways to make meetings even better next time around.

568 Practice Civility. Avoid offending by crudeness. No joke is worth insulting even *one* person in the meeting.

MISSION

569

The CONTEXT

of an invitation is

as important as

its CONTENT.

570 Develop A Mission Statement And Promote

It. For example, a mission statement developed by one school read: "Our goal is to create a positive environment where we believe each student is able, valuable, unique and a responsible human being. Students will be encouraged to succeed academically, socially, and emotionally with the cooperation of the faculty, staff, parents, and community." The mission statement of the International Alliance For Invitational Education is:A democratic society is ethically committed to seeing all people as able, valuable, and responsible, to valuing cooperation and collaboration, to viewing process as product in the making, and to developing untapped possibilities in all worthwhile areas of human endeavor.

Because the International Alliance For Invitational Education is dedicated to the perpetuation and enhancement of democratic principles, its mission is to enhance lifelong learning, promote positive change in organizations, cultivate the personal and professional growth and satisfaction of educators and allied professionals, and enrich the lives of human beings personally and professionally.

Invitational Education, a theory of practice, maintains that every person and everything in and around schools and other organizations adds to, or subtracts from, the process of being a beneficial presence in the lives of human beings. Ideally, the factors of people, places, policies, programs and processes should be so intentionally inviting as to create a world in which each individual is cordially summoned to develop intellectually, socially, physically, psychologically, and spiritually.

MORALE

571

An invitation is

an attitude

revealing itself.

572 **Plan A Teacher Appreciation Luncheon.** The parent council or PTA can sponsor a Teacher Appreciation luncheon to let teachers know that they are appreciated. It doesn't take much to put a bug in the right ear to make it happen. Usually this is done in May.

573 **Offer Mini-Grants.** It does not take a lot of money to provide seed grants to encourage creative classroom projects that will enhance the education of students. Outside groups, particularly business partners, can be asked to fund the mini-grants.

574 **Bake A Cake.** Teachers benefit from a home-like atmosphere. A freshly baked cake can do wonders to make the "recovery room" (teacher's lounge) more like a real home.

575 **Celebrate The New Arrival.** Invite all the faculty and staff to an after-school baby shower for a staff or faculty member who is expecting a new arrival. This is a very caring and supportive celebration of the growing school family.

576 **Organize A ROPES Course.** Few things are as effective at team building as a ROPES course. This course consists of overcoming fears and promoting teamwork by using ropes to master obstacles. This program is very popular with all sorts of businesses and is a great way to encourage teamwork in a school.

577 Show Appreciation For Extra Hours. There are many in school who because of their responsibilities spend extra hours in school long after the rest have gone. Coaches, drama teachers, music instructors, club sponsors all serve long hours, often under pressure. Show appreciation for their contribution through such things as a commendation from the school board or a faculty/staff recognition affair.

578 Salute The Leadership. Ask each staff member to write about one positive act accomplished by the principal which has seemed to make a difference in the school. Compile the comments into a letter of appreciation.

579 Initiate Service Pins. Service pins can be awarded for five, ten, fifteen, twenty, twenty-five years of service to the school system. These pins should be awarded to all members of the school family, including staff. These pins can be awarded during an assembly so that everyone can recognize those who have contributed so much to the school.

580 Hold An In-Service Breakfast. A faculty/staff breakfast on an in-service day will get things off to a great start. Be sure to invite any guests that may be making presentations at the in-service. This breakfast also helps to build a sense of togetherness for the school.

581 Maintain A Friendly Coffee Pot. Taking turns to prepare a fresh pot or urn of coffee in the teachers' lounge first thing each morning can be a wonderful morale booster.

582 Organize A Faculty Retreat. One of the best ways to boost morale is to plan a one-day faculty retreat in an attractive location other than the school. Campgrounds, resorts, and conference centers are all possibilities. The main thing is to break the mold and look at life through a different lens.

MOTIVATION

Author's note: According to Invitational Theory, motivation is an inherent component of individual functioning. Humans are not motivated from without, but rather are constantly and continually motivated from within. A student's or teacher's motivation may not be invested in the direction we would like, such as being conscientious in school work, but nonetheless the individual is always motivated. Our goal as educators is to direct a student's motivation toward goals we believe are in the best interests of the child. The following are examples of actions [blue cards] that can help direct a student's or teacher's motivation toward success in school

In Invitational Theory, these activities are referred to as dealing "blue cards." The blue and orange card metaphor represents the signals that occur between and among everyone who lives and works in a school. This signal system is both verbal and nonverbal and includes both language and paralanguage traits, such as tone and quality of voice.

Blue Cards. Blue cards carry the message that the person is able, valuable, and responsible. They encourage the individual to see the world as a good place to be, where there are many things to love that will love in return. Examples of blue cards would include asking someone to do something instead of telling them to do it, or encouraging someone to try something new.

Orange Cards. Orange cards inform the individual that he or she is unable, worthless, and irresponsible. An orange card warns the person to beware: Beware of one's own feelings, of relationships, of life. Orange cards are so painful that individuals will do almost anything to escape the hurt. Disregarding the comments of others concerning working conditions or change in job responsibilities can also be orange cards. Not saying hello when you pass a co-worker can be orange as well.

583 Paint The Room Blue.
Change the nature of the faculty lounge (workroom) to "family room." Paint it a pale blue to remind the faculty of its inviting function.

584 Paint The Blue Spot.
Paint the best parking spaces blue. Hold a drawing at each faculty meeting for these honored spaces.

585 Organize A Blue Crew.
Morale is always a concern in school. The Blue Crew can serve as a spirit club to keep school morale high.

586 Outline The Blue Route. Paint a special walking path around the school. Measure the path so that all members of the school community know how many laps equal one mile.

587 Send Blue Notes. Phrase feedback to others so that negative remarks are preceded by positive comments. For example, "Your work for the first three weeks was completed on time and your participation in class was very good. For the last three weeks your work has not been completed on time. I would like for you to complete your work on time for the next three weeks." Or, "I enjoy your energy level and curiosity in class and I would like for you to improve as a student by keeping focused on the class discussion rather than talking to the student seated next to you during class time."

588 Roost The Blue Bird. If students accomplish certain goals (improved SAT scores, attendance, or reading a certain number of books or pages), the principal will sit on the roof of the school for a morning.

589 Invent Ima Blue. Create an imaginary faculty or staff member who does nice things for the school. He or she may send a card or note of encouragement to faculty or staff or write a special holiday greeting. Ima also has her own mailbox. This activity often increases school morale.

590 Hold A Blue Hunt. Have a surprise scavenger hunt at a faculty meeting. Teachers are assigned to teams and each team is given one sheet of paper. Teachers are asked to find the items on the list within ten minutes. (The number of minutes left in the hunt is announced over the P.A. system.) Items that are blue get extra points. The team with the most points wins a prize.

591 Create Blue Readers. Students or faculty who read a certain number of books are recognized on a bulletin board near the main office and receive a blue ribbon book mark.

592 Give A Blue Bill. Tape a $1.00 bill (or other small gift wrapped in blue) under one chair to add to the excitement of a faculty meeting. This increases faculty attendance and faculty morale.

593 Draw A Blue Circle. Teachers circle misspelled words on papers. When a student turns in the paper with the correct spelling, the teacher adds a "K" so the paper reads "O.K."

594 Make A Link. Strips of blue paper are folded and made into links. Each link is inscribed with a student's success. The links form a chain around the classroom.

595 Use Blue Chalk. Teachers write on a chalk board with blue chalk a quote or statement for the day that encourages students to think and encourages them to work hard.

596 Invite The Blues Sisters. A group of female educators forms a chorus to "perform" at faculty meetings or PTA functions. The wackier the better.

597 Include The Blues Brothers. Same as above, but for males.

598 Identify Blue Ribbon Winners. Students who have improved the most in a certain area (grades, attendance, behavior in class, physical education class) are presented with blue ribbons to recognize their accomplishment.

599 Celebrate Blue Day. Everyone wears blue clothes to school on a designated day.

600 Award MBAs. Students receive recognition cards or stickers (such as "caught you being helpful") that indicate an attitude of helpfulness and consideration for others. The cards or stickers could read MBA—Major Blue Attitude.

601 **Give Blue Balloons.** Students who complete their homework assignments can enter their names in a drawing for a special blue balloon.

602 **Present Blue Hall Pass.** A student is rewarded for good behavior or performance by being allowed to leave class a few minutes early. Give these students a blue hall pass.

603 **Buy A Blue Bowl.** Obtain a bowl so students can write and drop in the names of classmates who do something thoughtful and caring for them. At the end of the week, the student whose name appears in the bowl the most gets special recognition.

604 **Paint A Blue Line.** Tape or paint a blue line across the school entrance doorway to remind everyone of the importance of politeness and respect in the school.

605 **Begin A Blue Suggestion Box.** Place a blue box in the school so that students, faculty, or staff might offer suggestions to improve the school.

606 **Hold "Blue Light Specials."** Sometime during the year, teachers or community leaders offer special classes at night, in the late afternoon or on a weekend that can be completed in three hours or less. Classes might include "How to Caulk a Window Frame," "Football: The Rules of The Games For Novices," "Parenting For School Success," "How To Make A Bird House Out of Everyday Items," "How The Blue Ridge Parkway Came To Be," "How To Use A Metal Detector," or "How To Make Chocolate Cookies."

607 **Wave Blue Bon Voyage.** When a student, faculty, or staff member is planning a trip to another country, ask students to come up with facts or information that might be helpful to the traveler.

MURALS

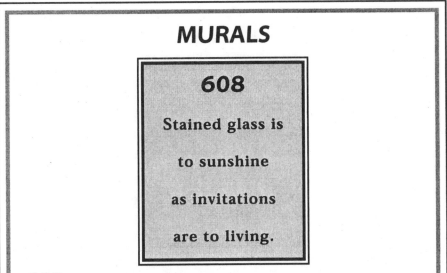

608

Stained glass is

to sunshine

as invitations

are to living.

609 **Create Classroom Murals.** Any blank wall in a classroom or school can be brightened with larger-than-life murals. Murals can be done on large sheets of white paper taped to the wall or on chalkboards. Use the opaque projector and a group of students with markers. The project teaches cooperation, and the beautiful results give students pride in their classroom.

610 **Paint Building Murals.** Hallways, clinics, dining areas, foyers, and gymnasiums can be enhanced with panels of murals depicting fantasy, history, or the school mascot. One group of students under the direction of the art teacher did a beautiful interpretation of King Arthur's Tales. The opaque projector is a great asset in painting murals.

611 **Celebrate Halloween.** Ask PTA members to find stores that will volunteer to display murals. The students design or make the murals in classroom or art class knowing in advance which store they will be decorating.

612 **Welcome Springtime.** On a warm, barefoot spring day, invite elementary students to dip their feet in a pan of water-soluble paint. Then have them make their footprints on a big sheet of paper. It will make an exciting and colorful painting. (And don't forget the teacher's and principal's feet.) "It is *our* classroom, *our* feet, and *our* mural."

MUSIC

> ## 613
>
> An invitation is
>
> measured both
>
> by its lyric
>
> and its melody.

614 **Play That Music.** Music is probably the second most important thing, aside from friendships, that students care about. Obtain a radio or cassette player for students to use at the beginning of homeroom or at break time. Educators get a turn too! It is an easy way to find out what students are listening to and might help educators find another avenue for communication.

615 **Sing A Commercial.** Randomly form the class into small groups and have each group select and sing a favorite TV commercial while converting the words to some academic concept. This helps stimulate learning by preventing boredom in the classroom.

616 **Share Folk Songs.** Many of today's youngsters do not have a background acquaintance with some of the good old-fashioned songs that many adults take for granted. Taking time to teach the class some of the folk songs that can be sung on the bus, at camp, or just for fun can develop classroom fellowship.

617 **Share The Talent.** Take every opportunity—at fine arts concerts, band festivals, local parades, and sports events—to let students perform. Bands, jazz units, and the chorus can also volunteer to perform at local shopping malls, nursing homes, and special event assemblies.

618 *Sing-Along.* One of the easiest ways to have a quick and effective assembly is to have a sing-along. Usually these are conducted around special holidays. However, if a week or season seems to be dragging, perhaps the music teacher can conduct an impromptu sing-along. The most effective way to make this a success is to have the principal lead the singing. Overhead transparencies add to the efficiency of the sing-along.

NAMES

> ## 619
>
> Is your invitation
>
> on a form letter,
>
> or is it
>
> handwritten?

620 **Use The Yearbook.** School yearbooks are a great source of names and faces. By spending some time looking through the yearbook and relating names to faces, faculty and staff will be in a better position to learn the names of many students in a relatively short time.

621 **Keep It Formal.** Insist that students address faculty and staff as "Mr., Mrs., Ms., or Dr." Students are expected to use last names. This requirement should also be maintained when students refer to other professionals in the school.

622 **Build Interest In Spelling.** A good way to combine social relationships with basic spelling skills is to use the first name of each child in spelling lists. This encourages students to get to know each other while learning how to spell.

623 Share Names. A way to reduce threat at the beginning of the year is to encourage students to learn more about each other. To do this the teacher may ask students to tell others in the group about their name. For example, "For whom were you named?" "What does your name mean?" "Does your name seem to fit you?" "Do you like your name?" or "What do you like to be called?" When handled appropriately, this simple ice-breaker invites students to talk about themselves in a nonthreatening manner.

624 Check Etymologies. Encourage students to see if they can find the origins of their names in etymology reference books.

625 Be A Name-Dropper. When necessary to focus a student's attention on the lesson, use his or her name in the context of the lesson. For example, "Charlie, do you think that the author was too judgmental about this character?" or "Betty, how do you think the heroine felt?" This "low-card" approach encourages students to keep their attention on the lesson content.

626 Keep A Mug File. Start a card file on members of the school's professional family, including teachers, aides, custodians, cafeteria staff, bus drivers, counselors—every adult who serves the school system. A single index card can hold a wealth of information about people. On each card list personal items, such as name of spouse, number of children, hobbies, and interests. From time to time go through the file and add information.

627 Learn Handles. People respond best when they are called by their preferred name. Take time to learn the correct pronunciation and use the preferred name at every opportunity. Calling people by their preferred name shows interest and caring.

NATURE TRAIL

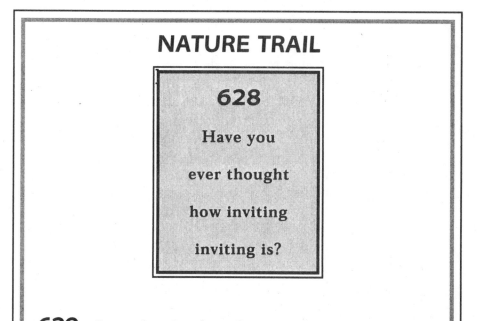

628

Have you

ever thought

how inviting

inviting is?

629 **Organize Student Rangers.** Should the school be fortunate to have a nature trail, organize student rangers to serve as guides to enable students from throughout the area to visit, study, and learn more about the natural beauty of their area. A trail covered with wood chips helps. The areas must be policed.

NEW FACULTY-STAFF

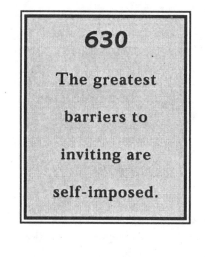

630

The greatest

barriers to

inviting are

self-imposed.

631 **Join The Club.** Help beginning teachers in every way possible. This help might include an orientation program, information about what is available in the school, and special recognition to welcome new teachers. This recognition can include having the first edition of the student newspaper or school bulletin focus exclusively on the new teachers.

632 **Organize Partner Teachers.** When a new teacher comes into the building, it is advantageous to assign a mentor teacher to show that new person the ropes. It allows the new teacher to have someone to rely on for little individual things that happen in the building. In some cases, it helps to assign a mentor teacher to a brand new teacher for instructional purposes. Some schools use master teachers to accomplish this goal.

633 **Embrace The New Teacher.** While the administration usually acquaints new teachers with "policies," experienced faculty and staff can also meet with new teachers to give them a "survival manual" of practical suggestions and words of comfort to help make their lives more endurable during that first year.

634 **Organize A Back-To-School Faculty-Staff Party.** Renew friendships, introduce new colleagues, and set the stage for the coming year. Invite everyone to bring a covered dish and enjoy an evening of fun.

NEW SCHOOL YEAR

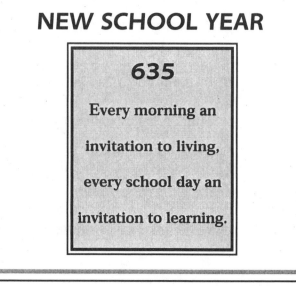

635

Every morning an invitation to living, every school day an invitation to learning.

636 **Be A Show-Off.** Summers offer time for maintenance personnel to paint walls, strip and wax floors, and generally get things ready for the new school year. Take the opportunity at the very beginning of the school year to have an open-house program to show off the sparkling building.

637 **Express Your Pleasure.** At the beginning of the new year, why not tell your students how pleased and honored you are to share their company during the semester? The students may never have heard this from a teacher before. It will bowl them over, and you're off to a good school year.

638 **Phone Introductions.** Sometime during the beginning of the new school year, teachers can call as many parents as possible to introduce themselves and welcome their children to the new school year. This gets the year off to a great start.

639 **Create A Helping Hands Chart.** Plan the classroom responsibilities together the first day of school. *Everyone* has a job which is rotated each week.

640 **Get A Jump Start.** First grade children come to school the first day very excited, expecting to learn to read and write. Don't disappoint them. Duplicate a very simple, brief paragraph story with several blanks. "I go to _____ school. My teacher's name is _____." Write the answers on the board and let them practice. Students can take their papers home and exclaim, "I learned to read and write today!"

641 **Develop Class Spirit.** At the beginning of the school year invite the class to decide upon a name for the group. The class might also select a motto and class colors. These can be used on the outside of the classroom door, for displays, and on messages. By using the same techniques as an athletic team, a class can develop real team spirit.

642 **Plan A Treasure Map.** Distribute maps of the school to insure that everyone knows how to get around the school. Along with the map distribute lists of special activities, organizations, and programs that are open to all students.

643 **Hold A News Conference.** Before school begins, hold a "press review" with media people from local newspapers, radio, and television. Invite them for coffee and a quick look at what the school is planning for the year. Of course, this should be an organized group effort and approved by the central office.

644 **Launch A Media Blitz.** Feature spot announcements or messages in newspapers or airways saying that the school welcomes all students to a new and exciting school year. Make the ads enthusiastic. Students can be a great help with this.

645 **Write Special Notes.** As soon as the class roster is available and before students return to school after summer break, mail a letter or card to each student welcoming him or her to school. A handwritten note is far superior to a form letter.

646 **Send Welcome Back Letters.** A welcome back letter is sent home from the school two weeks before school starts. It highlights when school starts and gives important information for students and parents. Have students write their own address on an envelope in late spring. The expense of a first-class stamp is well worth it. It lets parents know that the school is on the job working and preparing for their children.

647 **Organize First Day Parent Guides.** Parents active in the school make wonderful guides and helpers the first day of school. Given lists of all classes, they can help students find their classroom, reassure the insecure, or bring to the office the student who has gotten off the bus at the wrong school. A room supplied with coffee and cookies can be available for parents on the first day of school. This is particularly helpful for parents of kindergarten children when both the child and parents are having trouble letting go.

648 Give Opening Day Apples. We've all heard of an "Apple for the Teacher." Well, switch things around, and on opening day of school have an apple on the desk of each student in each class. This can be a specific way of saying: "How glad we are to have you here, and how much we will learn together this year."

649 Form Bus Buddies. Volunteer parents ride kindergarten buses the first three days of school to insure children get off the bus at the correct bus stop. If there is no parent to receive the child, he or she is brought back to school. No child is returned to an empty home.

650 Have Student Leader Greeters. Arrange for student leaders to serve as greeters and tour guides on the first day of school. They can escort new students to their new classrooms and introduce them to their new teachers. This invites everyone to feel special.

651 Prime The Pump. Initial contacts with students are very important. Before school starts call or send a postcard to each incoming student. Welcome the student to *our* school and offer a summer registration tour for all new students and their families. Invitations can start early.

652 Set The Atmosphere. It is important to set the right atmosphere the first minutes of the new school year. Have greeters at the school entrance *and* classroom door, and let newcomers know how pleased and honored the school is to have the pleasure of their company, and that the school is looking forward to working with them. Build positive relationships early.

653 Hold A "Young Parents Tea Party." Parents who are sending a child to school for the first time often have fears and anxieties about "losing" their children. It can be most helpful if these parents are invited to tea and shown what their children will experience. This is also an excellent way to recruit parent volunteers.

654 **Plan A Back-To-School Picnic.** Having a picnic that involves parents, students, and teachers prior to the opening of school is an outstanding way to start the year. The main problem with this is organization. However, the schools that have the back-to-school picnics find that they are outstanding social events. They are generally run by the PTA or PTO.

655 **Do Not Forward.** This is a simple trick that lets the school know exactly who has moved over the summer. Send a general welcome letter to every household approximately two weeks before school starts. Put a label on the lower left hand corner of the envelope that says "PLEASE DO NOT FORWARD." Any family member who has moved from an address will not receive this piece of mail. It will be returned by the post office to the school. This lets the school know exactly who has moved, and is extremely helpful in planning class lists prior to the opening of school.

656 **Employ Flower Power.** At the beginning of the new school year, obtain an inexpensive flower vase for each faculty and staff member's desk. Place one flower in each vase on Monday morning before anyone arrives. Keep the tradition going throughout the school year. Student clubs or parent volunteers can help with the task, and flowers can be obtained wholesale through some friendly nursery or flower shop. The cost per flower is measured in pennies, and there is a significant impact on morale.

657 **Show And Tell.** When done caringly and appropriately, "show and tell" works well with any group of students. Ask students: "Among your personal treasures, what is there that says something about you?" Invite students to bring their mementos to school and share them during a "sharing" session. By talking about their treasures, they are really talking about themselves. It is an effective way to get students to know each other at the beginning of the new school year.

NEWSLETTERS

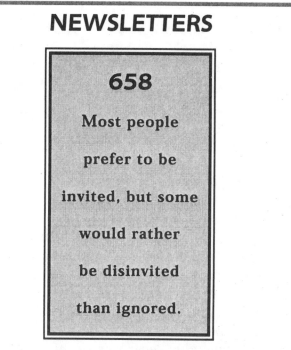

658

Most people

prefer to be

invited, but some

would rather

be disinvited

than ignored.

659 Piggy Back The Newsletter. A quarterly newsletter can be sent with the report cards to every student's parents. These newsletters can also be distributed to business and community leaders to keep everyone informed of upcoming school events.

660 Number The Newsletters. Newsletters sent home with students or mailed can be given a number corresponding to a student name. Announce to all students that one week after the newsletters are sent home, the school will select one parent at random and will call the home. If the parent has (1) received the newsletter, and (2) read the newsletter and can answer a question or two, then the entire class receives a prize (pizza lunch, ice cream, etc.). It is a good way to insure that newsletters get home and are read!

661 Spotlight The Alumni. Use the school newsletter to accent significant achievements by students who have attended the school. It does not have to be a regular section, but can be added when an outstanding award or achievement has been accomplished by a former student. Examples might include: all-state recognition, honor society, honor roll, or any other awards that former students have received.

NEWSPAPERS

662 **Publish A School Newspaper.** The school newspaper is a great way to communicate special activities, awards, upcoming events, and *good* news about the school. This newspaper can be sent to local public officials, retired employees and shared among schools. It is also helpful to exchange newspapers with other schools. Be sure to include student artwork and writing in the school paper.

663 **Create A Class Newspaper.** A class newspaper can be organized and managed by students as part of the language-arts program. Students can print, illustrate, and circulate their paper to friends and to families to let everyone know of class happenings.

664 **Use The Newspaper.** Watch the local newspaper for articles dealing with students and families, and their interests. Clipping newspaper articles and sharing them with students—even sending a holiday or other special greeting to the class by placing a classified ad in the local paper—can be effective both as a means of expressing positive feelings and as a way of encouraging students to read.

665 **Spread Good News.** Prepare a weekly column in the local newspaper to highlight school activities, special accomplishments, education ideas, and to educate the public generally about the good things taking place in schools. Other forms of mass communication, including radio and television programs, should not be overlooked.

666 **Encourage Newspaper Features.** Call the local paper to take pictures or do an article about a special activity happening in the school. Students and parents love to see things about their school in the paper. Some papers will even feature student work (art, compositions, etc.). The newspaper generally will not send a reporter to the school without a special invitation.

667 Know The Editor. Without news a newspaper is out of business. Most local newspapers have a person who is responsible for news in schools. Get to know this person and put him or her on a mailing list for the school newsletters.

668 Run An Ad. Send a holiday or other special greeting to students (or colleagues) by placing a classified ad in the local newspaper. Set the stage by hinting that something very special will appear in the newspaper in the next few days. Students will study the paper to discover that "special" something.

669 Enlist A Parent. A parent can act as a public relations person for the school and maintain contact with the local newspaper. This is particularly effective when the parent has professional experience in the newspaper business.

NEW STUDENTS

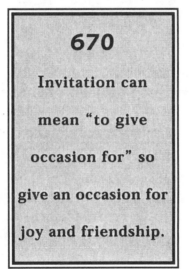

670

Invitation can

mean "to give

occasion for" so

give an occasion for

joy and friendship.

671 Recognize New Students. When a new student enrolls in the school, find out a few pertinent and positive things, such as what town the student is coming from, personal interests, whether or not the student is an athlete or club member, and where the student resides now. Then introduce the student to the class and share (with student's permission) these positive tidbits of information.

672 Obtain Principal Pencils. Have a box of pencils with the principal's or headmaster's name stamped on them along with the saying "From Your Principal." This will immediately allow the students to know the principal *via* name association. They will have something that none of the other students in the school have. It is also a great hit with new parents.

673 Send Family Welcome Letters. To develop rapport between new families and the school have a standard typed letter which can be sent approximately two to three weeks after a new student is enrolled. This follow-up letter reminds parents that they are a valued part of the school community. Each school tailors its comments to fit its setting, the grade of the student enrolled, and upcoming special events.

674 Organize A Buddy System. Establish a system in which each new student is assigned a "Peer Buddy" and a "Teacher Buddy." These buddies make a special effort to show the new student the ropes, introduce them to others, and help them with assignments. This is an excellent policy with any new student, but is particularly helpful with "at-risk" or homeless students.

675 Welcome Wagon Bags. Develop a project based on the National Welcome Wagon Organization. This project includes a bag full of coupons for each new student. Each coupon is redeemable for a small gift. The bag contains a map, all necessary school information, plus information from the PTA/PTO.

676 Write A "New Student Handbook." This booklet could be titled: "Everything You Need to Know About Your New School, But Are Too Shy to Ask." This would be a booklet written by students for students who are new to the district. It describes the school and offers advice from the student's side of the desk.

677 **Play "Gossip."** To encourage new students, play a fun game called "Gossip." Whisper a message in the ear of the nearest student who in turn whispers it to the next student. Watch the changes. All students enjoy the game and new students easily become a part of a group.

OFFICES

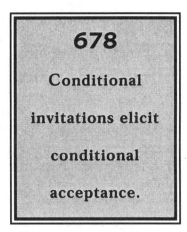

678

Conditional

invitations elicit

conditional

acceptance.

679 **Keep The Office Alive.** A bright, cheerful, and clean office with comfortable chairs offers a pleasant, non-verbal message about the quality of life in a school. Outer offices can be made more attractive by hanging live plants and having up-to-date reading materials available.

680 **Maintain A Toy Box.** A toy box is an absolute necessity for every principal's office at any level. Purchase $10 to $15 worth of small toys such as animal figures, little cars, or farmyard figures. These items should be easily accessible to the principal when a parent comes in with a preschooler. There are numerous times when conferences with parents last more than five minutes. A preschooler's attention span is quite short. Also, a child of this age will most likely wander around the office. By providing toys to occupy the child's time, the parents and principal can meet undisturbed.

681 **Provide A Sick Room Or Be Prepared For Illness.** A bed should be made available for students who are too ill to return to class. The attendance office, secretary, or nurse should immediately telephone the student's parents or guardian.

682 **Arrange A Visitor Center.** Where possible, rearrange the office to include an informal area where visitors can be seated for conversation. Comfortable chairs, a coffee table, fresh-cut flowers, and an area rug can do wonders for any area.

683 **Declare War On Counters.** Many schools have a heavy counter in the main office. This counter serves as a clear barrier for visitors. A better approach is to have a receptionist desk where visitors can be greeted and given information as needed.

684 **Open The Office To Learning.** The school offices provide a great place for students to learn about office careers. Encourage students to volunteer to work in the office and learn what it is like to be a professional office worker.

685 **Keep Lots Of Facial Tissues.** Boxes of Kleenex are a must in every office. They can be valuable in any small emergency, including runny noses, tears, and mopping up little messes.

686 **Arrange Invitational Furniture.** Furniture can be a wonderful addition or a clear drawback to any office. Here are three simple rules to follow: (1) Chairs in the office should be the same size and type (no "throne" for the administrator); (2) Decorations should be understated so that the visitor can feel comfortable, and (3) A discussion area should be available where there are no barriers between administrator and visitor.

PARKING

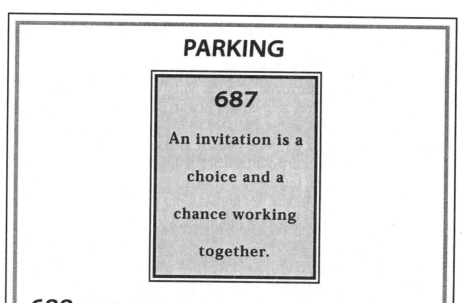

687

An invitation is a choice and a chance working together.

688 Mark The Spot. Designate a special parking spot (close to the entrance) with blue paint. On Friday afternoon, before the staff leaves, a lottery is held to pick the staff member who will get to park there for one full week.

689 Insure Convenient Guest And Visitor Parking. Provide parking spaces conveniently located near the office for guests and visitors. A sign indicating a "welcome" to visitors and guests can be placed to mark these special parking spaces.

PATRIOTISM

690 Salute Patriotism. Students can take turns raising the flag each day. This arrangement teaches students a sense of responsibility and encourages a feeling of patriotism.

691 Invite A Hero. Invite a war veteran, public official, or world traveler to talk with the class about his or her experiences in other countries, nations, or provinces. The guest could discuss differences and similarities among cultures visited.

PETS

692 Bring On The Empty Horses. Organize a pet show for the class, a group of classes, or the entire school. Invite students to bring their pets to school (with parent approval and support). Everything from frogs to horses will show up. It makes for an exciting school day and an excellent opportunity to teach responsible behavior with pets.

693 Select a Classroom Pet. Obtain a hardy little animal and create an environmentally comfortable world for it—for example, a large aquarium for a small turtle, with a warm rock for sunbathing and a little pool for swimming. One classroom has an iguana with its own ladder that allows it to climb up on the window sill and enjoy the view. Teachers supervise students in the care for their pet.

694 Support a Mascot. Invite the class to select (by vote) a class mascot and organize a class fund-raiser (collect aluminum cans or hold a bake sale). Choose a way to use the funds to further a humane project for the chosen pet.

PHOTOGRAPHY

695 Appoint A Photographer. Every school should have a good camera and operator to take pictures of significant things that happen around school. The camera also can be used by the principal or other member of the school family to take pictures of students who have done outstanding work. Have two prints made of each photo. One print is given to the person who collects materials for the scrapbook or heritage room and the other is sent home via U.S. mail with a short note from the principal. That picture will become one of the most valued pictures the family will collect.

696 **Be A Camera Bug.** Take pictures of new students and place them on the bulletin board or in the front hallway. Include a message about the student and any hobbies or interests he or she has.

697 **Take Celebrity Photos.** Arrange a "Lunch with the Principal" program where students are selected by various means (nominations for improved behavior, recognitions for accomplishments) to attend a special luncheon with the principal. A photograph is taken of the principal and student enjoying lunch together and sent home to parents. A copy is also given to the student.

698 **Take A Class Photograph.** Take a group photograph of the class early in the school year and place it in a visible location. Look back on it as the year progresses and take another photograph the last week of school. Everyone will be amazed at the changes.

699 **Display The Photograph.** Sometimes during staff meetings or teacher/parent conferences the student under consideration becomes some abstract "problem." Keep a human face in the equation by displaying a photograph of the student on the table for all to see and remember that a unique human is behind the label.

PLAYGROUNDS

700

Springtime

invites a

celebration

in the heart.

701 Schedule Playground Projects. It is essential to update and double-check playground equipment regularly. A good way to do this is to have a playground project committee. Its role may be as small as doing some landscaping, or as large as obtaining a major playground set. It is important to have a project each year. Parents and community are useful allies as the project progresses.

702 Invite Business Partners. Contact businesses in the community to participate in playground projects. Businesses who contribute time and/or money to improve the equipment and landscaping of the playground are recognized by small plaques or signs placed in the playground.

703 Hold A Playground Party. One way to raise money for improving playgrounds is to sponsor a barbeque, chicken dumpling supper, or fish fry for the community. Publicize it well ahead and contact businesses to donate food or money. Later, hold an open house and ribbon cutting for the new, improved playground.

POLICIES

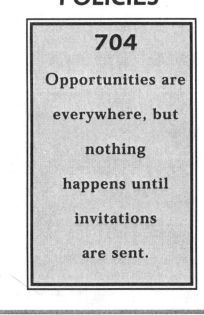

704

Opportunities are

everywhere, but

nothing

happens until

invitations

are sent.

705 Be Explicit. The more explicit an invitation, the more it lends itself to acceptance. Sometimes educators create misunderstandings by being vague with their policies. Others wonder "What did they mean by that?" When invitations are explicit the likelihood of success increases.

706 Invite Action. Too often, policies give directions that could best be followed by pet rocks: "*Don't* leave a class unattended," "*No* smoking in the school," "*Cease* posting political posters in the school." Under such directions a pet rock would make an ideal educator! Policies which invite action are much better than ones that require inaction.

707 Keep Rules Short & Simple. Such simple rules as (1) Please follow directions, (2) Please respect property, (3) Please speak softly, and (4) Please be courteous, can do wonders to maintain good student behavior. The fewer the rules, the less likely rules will be broken.

708 Look For Causes. Sometimes difficulties in and around the schools are caused by policies rather than people. For example, scheduling buses to leave school within minutes after school ends forces students to run, shove, and push to make the bus. Changing the policy may eliminate the problem.

709 Communicate Clearly. Policies can be conveyed with posters in every classroom, in student grade-level meetings, staff meetings, and PTO meetings. They can be posted in and around schools, and sent home to parents and to local businesses. Ample communication about policies assures a good understanding of them.

710 Remember SPCA. All rules and policies should be stated:

> **S**imply (Complexity is the natural enemy of comprehension).

> **P**ositively (The focus is on what should be done, not what should not be done).

> **C**onsistently (Everyone is consistent in enforcing the rules).

> **A**ffirmatively (Emphasize the good, not the bad).

711 Work To Eliminate Ultimatums. Include everyone who is influenced by a policy to be a part of the policy-making process. Make sure that "our" policies are really *ours*.

PRESENTATIONS

712 Be Relevant. Work to make the presentation as relevant as possible to the place, date, and time, as well as to the group in the audience.

713 Be Brief. Resist to the death the temptation to be long. Keep on schedule and end on time.

714 Be Comfortable. When the presenter is comfortable it is likely that the audience will be, too. Take it easy and the audience will follow.

715 Be Friendly. While waiting to begin, try to chat with as many participants as possible. This helps to break the ice.

716 Talk From Experience. A great method to underscore the major points of a presentation is to use examples from one's own life.

717 Go Heavy With Handouts. A good way to insure that the presentation has solid content is to prepare informational packets for distribution to the audience.

718 Encourage Discussion. People at presentations like to talk as well as listen. An open question and answer period can be valuable, as can breaking the audience into informal "buzz" groups to talk about what has been presented.

719 Hang In There. Audiences don't mind seeing a presenter get a little rattled or confused if the presenter keeps marching. Never give up in front of an audience.

720 Use Silence. Develop the confidence to wait. People need time to reflect on what has been presented.

721 Watch That Environment. An ineffective mike, improper lighting, limited visibility, room seating arrangement, even room temperature or time of day can make or break any speaker. *Insist* that the physical environment be as inviting as possible.

PROFESSIONAL DEVELOPMENT

722

When an invitation is accepted and good things happen, the likelihood that future invitations will be accepted is enhanced.

7.23 Join Professional Groups. Be active in professional societies and seek certification. Working within these organizations insures that they maintain high professional quality. This strengthens the profession and oneself.

724 Schedule Teacher Ex-changes. Organize a program in which teachers from different schools can take turns swapping classrooms for a day. Alternatively, provide substitute coverage from school funds to allow teachers to visit exemplary schools and observe other teachers.

725 Hold A One-Minute Work-shop. Ask each member of the faculty/staff to present a one-minute program on a particular topic, such as "My best teaching tip" or the "Most important thing I learned as a professional." Ideas presented are those which can be used by everyone.

726 Upgrade In-Service Programs. Survey the faculty and staff for suggested topics and speakers that will address the real concerns of school professionals. For example, "Understanding the adolescent personality," "Maintaining good discipline," and "Demonstrating teaching techniques that work" are usually popular with teachers when presented well.

727 Organize A Professional Library. Every school should have a professional library. Ideally, the library should be in the faculty workroom or lounge for convenient access. Include books on Invitational Education. A list is available by writing Invitational Education, c/o School of Education, University of North Carolina at Greensboro, Greensboro, NC 27412.

728 Write For Publication. A valuable way to become involved professionally is to write for professional publications. Your article does not have to appear in national journals to be a helpful contribution to the profession. There are numerous local, state, and regional newsletters, journals, and related publications that welcome contributions from educators in the field.

729 **Bring Home The Bacon.** When faculty or staff members attend a workshop or conference, arrange for them to be available as a speaker to give a brief overview of what they learned. They can also duplicate the materials they received at the conference and distribute these to school colleagues.

730 **Share The Consultant.** For an in-service program, invite neighboring systems or related organizations to share the cost of bringing in a consultant or well-known speaker. It makes good money sense, saves travel time for the consultant, and invites a feeling of cooperation with other systems and agencies.

731 **Swap A Teacher.** Arrange to trade positions with a teacher from another school for a week. This will enrich everyone— the school, the teacher who volunteers to participate, and the students involved. It is a good way to avoid the early spring "blahs."

732 **Carpool An Adventure.** If an important conference, a noted lecturer, or a training workshop is scheduled in a nearby city, join with colleagues, pool your gas money, and attend as a group. Enjoy the companionship going and coming. While there, pick up brochures, handouts, and good ideas to share with colleagues back home.

733 **Give A Professional Gift.** Need a gift for a special friend or a prize to be given for some special event? Subscribe to a professional magazine or journal to be sent to him or her. It's a gift that keeps on giving.

734 **Rip And Read.** The busy professional does not have time to read all the articles in newspapers, magazines and journals. Therefore, scan a publication and rip out what is useful. The rest can be recycled.

PROFESSIONALISM

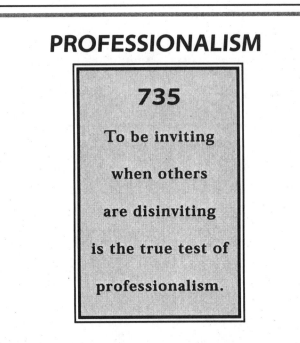

735

To be inviting

when others

are disinviting

is the true test of

professionalism.

736 Participate In Programs. In addition to typical academic courses, programs, and degrees, there are special conferences and workshops that can provide exciting ways to sharpen skills, learn techniques, and develop new understandings. Attending such professional activities will help one upgrade skills and knowledge.

737 Be A Booster. The educator's time is severely limited, but his or her presence at a play, a band concert, an athletic contest, or other student activity can be seen as a most inviting act. When students (and parents) perceive the school professional as interested in their activities, they will probably feel more invited by the school.

738 Rejuvenate Professionalism. Attend a regional or state education conference, even if for only one day. And remember, good learning can occur at both formal sessions and informal gatherings—like happy hour!

739 Venture An Invitation. There may be someone in your professional world whom you would like to know better. Give it an honest shot and invite that person to lunch one day.

(Your dearest friend in all the world was once a total stranger. And the friendship began with an invitation.)

740 Be Professionally Responsible.
An important way to improve the quality of life in school is to be ethically responsible. Be trustworthy with confidences, follow rules, or, if they are bad rules, work to change them, and support colleagues and the organization.

741 Follow Through Promptly.
One of the most significant characteristics of the professional person is that he or she follows through promptly. The most positive action, when long delayed, loses much of its reward value.

742 Encourage Professional Dress.
The best way to be treated professionally is to "walk your talk." When educators come to school each day, they should look like they're going somewhere important. The best way to encourage professional dress in the school is to serve as a model for colleagues.

743 Promote Civility.
Common courtesy is a most important tool of the inviting educator. This is usually accomplished by greeting others by name, showing respect by being prompt with appointments and commitments, promoting "please" and "thank you," and, in general, showing basic concern and appreciation for others and their feelings.

744 Carry Business Cards.
Many educators carry business cards. A real treat for teachers is for the school to provide a set of business cards for them. The initial outlay is somewhat expensive; however, after this is done, buying cards for new staff members is very inexpensive. It is a way to remind teachers that they are professionals and that they should be proud of their profession.

745 **Spend Time Reading.** There are countless professional books, journals, magazine articles, newsletters, monographs, and the like that are expressly written to help educators develop professionally. Finding some time each day to read is an excellent way to stay abreast of new ideas.

746 **Visit Another World.** Make time to explore other settings, such as businesses, industry, hospitals, clinics, or other work settings that are different from one's own to see how people do things. Professional knowledge takes many forms, and there are good ideas to be collected and put to good use in the school.

747 **Take Time To Think.** Writing a brief article for a journal takes time, but it's a rewarding experience to take time to capture ideas on paper. There are exciting things happening in every school that are worth an article or two.

748 **Conduct Research.** Some educators might assume that research should be left to scientists in laboratories, surrounded by computers and data sheets. But bigger is not necessarily better. A teacher's quiet investigation of some question can have a long-range influence.

749 **Admit Ignorance.** Instead of struggling to know everything, take time to say "I don't know." Follow this up with "What do you think?" The other person will be impressed that he or she was asked.

750 **Develop The I. Q. (Invitational Quotient).** Some practical ways to help make the school more inviting include:
- Joining the International Alliance For Invitational Education.
- Obtaining books and materials on Invitational Education for the school library.
- Applying for the Inviting School Award.
- Attending Invitational Education conferences and workshops.

751 **Make Decisions Expeditiously.** The longer a decision is put off, the more difficult it is to make. It also lessens the amount of time available to correct wrong decisions. Even if the decision is wrong it can be a valuable learning experience that leads to adjustment and correction.

752 **Promote The Territory.** When your invitations are accepted, be sure to do everything you can to insure that the acceptance results in positive experience. Follow up promptly and be responsible for what takes place after the invitation has been extended and accepted.

753 **Keep The Faith.** It is important that the professional not lose heart in the face of rejection. If an invitation is sent it may or may not be accepted, but if it is not sent then it cannot be accepted. For this and other reasons, keep on marching. Sometimes a little *patience* and *persistence* can make all the difference.

754 **Give "Expert" Advice Sparingly.** One of the basic tenets of Invitational Education is to recognize that every person has the potential of becoming more capable and self-supportive. For this reason be reluctant in providing the "ready" answer for problems. To provide answers can be disinviting because such behavior can suggest that the person is incapable of making appropriate decisions for him or herself.

755 **Be Stainless Steel.** One of the marvels of steel is that it can bend without breaking. Practice being flexible under stress, and seek to find alternatives and ways to bend without breaking. In other words, roll with the punches.

756 **Join The Alliance.** One good way to keep the invitational momentum going in a school is to join the International Alliance For Invitational Education. Membership provides the

Invitational Education Forum, advance notices of invitational conferences and workshops, and *The Journal of Invitational Theory and Practice.* For details regarding membership, write the Alliance, c/o School of Education, University of North Carolina at Greensboro, Greensboro, NC 27412.

757 Control Waste. Wasted supplies, utilities, and materials take valuable resources away from the real needs of the school. Hold a contest on ways to control wasted resources in and around the school.

PROGRAMS

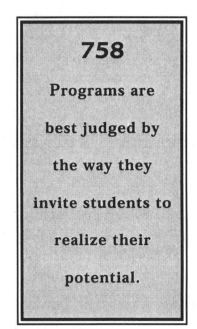

758

Programs are

best judged by

the way they

invite students to

realize their

potential.

759 Keep A Level Playing Field. When one area (such as sports) is recognized, be sure that other activities in the school are equally recognized. To celebrate one activity and neglect others is very disinviting.

760 **Play Fair.** Some students have disabilities that prevent them from participating in the activities that other students enjoy. Provide opportunities for these students to participate in extra-curricular activities Wheelchair students could have a ping pong or tennis tournament, etc. which is recognized with as much enthusiasm as events sponsored for students without these disabilities. This encourages all students to feel that they are a part of the school.

761 **Lend An Ear To Students.** When planning programs, it is helpful to keep up with what topics or activities are important to students. Listen to the ideas students have about what programs they want or feel are needed at the school. It is always a challenge to keep informed about the mindset of each class of students that enters school. Each has unique needs arising from societal and generational changes.

PUBLIC ADDRESS
(P.A.) SYSTEM

762

The right

invitation at

the right time

can turn a frog

into a prince.

763 **Ration the P.A. System.** Interruptions rank among the biggest frustrations of teachers. Use of the P.A. system should be severely limited to the first five or last five minutes of the school day, except for emergencies. It has been estimated that every time the P.A. comes on, seven minutes of classroom learning for every student is cancelled.

764 **Improve P.A. Quality.** Test the public address system for sound quality. How does it sound in various parts of the building? The sound quality can be improved by speaking in a normal voice. There is no need to shout or swallow the mike.

765 **Use Student Announcers.** Whether it is to lead the Pledge of Allegiance, offer morning news, or make announcements, students can be selected to serve as announcers. They usually enjoy speaking over the P.A. system and with a little bit of coaching can do a good job. This can be a special thrill for "at-risk" students.

766 **Hold Educational Trivia Contests.** During morning announcements, squeeze in an educational trivia contest or even a scavenger hunt. This keeps student (and teacher) interest during the announcement process.

767 **Encourage Students To Express Their Creativity.** Students of any age enjoy sharing short poems or jokes on the P.A. system. This is especially a treat for elementary school children.

QUESTIONS

768 **Use Zen Koans.** Zen masters use a special kind of question to invite their students to reflect deeply about oneself and one's relationship with the world. A koan is a simple question that has no simple answer. For example: "What is the sound of one hand clapping?" "What is love?" It is the student's struggle with the koan, rather than the teaching of the master, that enlightens the student.

769 **Open-End The Questions.** By asking questions that require more than a *yes* or *no* answer, the teacher invites discussion and dialogue. For example, "What do you think about..." or "How would you describe..." generates higher-order thinking skills and student involvement.

770 **Invite Questions.** Often the "Are there any questions?" approach is simply a sign that the teacher is ready to move to the next point. To elicit questions, try this: "I'm not sure we've got this point down pat; does anybody share my concern?" Or this: "I think I've left some gaps in this explanation; would you help me identify what I've missed?" These comments are much more likely to generate questions.

771 **Invite Dialogue.** Explain to students that "It's not the answers to my questions that are important, but the *questions* you have for my *answers*." Knowledge is constantly unfolding, and today's accepted fact may soon become tomorrow's outmoded concept. By challenging ideas, students grow intellectually.

RESTROOMS

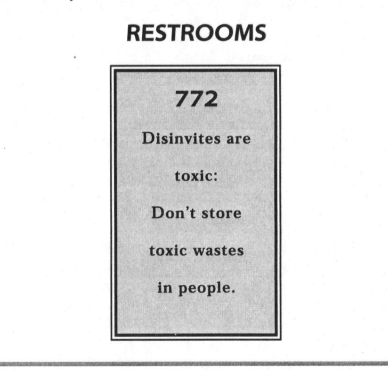

772

Disinvites are

toxic:

Don't store

toxic wastes

in people.

773 Design Restful Restrooms. Perhaps nothing in a school speaks louder about the philosophy of the school than student bathrooms. Are they clean, dignified, and are soap, towels, and tissue in all restrooms? Is there a degree of privacy, including stall doors? The important point is not to let vandals run the school. If a door is broken, or mirror shattered, replace it quickly while actively searching for the offenders.

774 Help The Aim. For younger boys who miss the mark at the urinal, a black painted dot may help with keeping a more pleasant boys' restroom.

SAFETY

775 Have Everyone Tag Up. Order attractive metal name tags for everyone who works in and around the school, including all faculty and staff. Name tags have long been used by helpers in other professions, including health care, law enforcement, airline travel, and customer services in business. While they are a minor inconvenience to some, name tags are a great help to substitute teachers, visitors, and new students. Tags identify all professionals in the school and help to promote general security.

776 Call The Cops. A law enforcement officer perks up any meeting. The sight of a uniform is usually sufficient to think seriously about safety in and around schools. Invite a law enforcement official to share some do's and don'ts regarding safety.

777 Sponsor Bicycle Safety Inspections. Have the students organize a "bicycle safety inspection" for their grade level by contacting the local police department and making arrangements to have an officer assist them. These organizers will feel more responsible while adding to the safety of themselves and others.

778 **Hold A Bicycle Safety Rodeo.** Teachers conduct safety instruction before the rodeo. The rodeo is held on a Saturday morning, and an assembly is held the following Monday with a guest speaker from the State Police, Sheriff's office, or local police. A drawing is held for bicycle accessories. Certificates of participation are given to each student who attends the rodeo. (Ask local bicycle stores to help.)

779 **Send A Home Safety Checklist.** Devise cooperatively a home safety checklist that will be manageable for students. Urge the students to take the inventory home to review with a parent or guardian, to be returned for a "Safety Inspector" award—perhaps signed by the teacher and the principal. The students feel valuable and responsible for having helped make their homes safer places to live. The home and school connection is strengthened as parents are involved.

780 **Form A School Safety Committee.** This committee can work to ensure the safety and security of everyone in the school. The committee can consider such issues as a smoke-free school, the use of students in handling heavy or dangerous equipment, the removal of chains or other exit obstructions, and emergency procedures.

781 **Present A Fire Danger Awareness Program.** In addition to having normal fire drills and celebrating fire prevention week, schools can arrange for local firefighters to bring a fire truck to school for a safety demonstration. This can be accompanied by an essay/poster contest. It is important to compliment students after an orderly fire drill or good behavior at a safety demonstration.

782 **Watch The Weather.** Keep alert for weather conditions throughout the school day. Use the P.A. system or messengers to inform everyone in the school of hazardous road conditions or serious weather advisories before they leave school.

783 Locate The First Aid Kit. It is important for teachers, students, and staff to know where they can find a first aid kit when injuries occur. It helps to know where bandages or medicines for cuts and insect bites are located. This is particularly true if the school does not have a nurse.

784 Conduct A Safety Check. While there are various "official" safety checks of the school building by fire marshals and others experts, it is a good idea for educators to do a thorough safety check for the entire building and look for potential hazards. Educators know the most about the day-to-day use of the building and should have a special lookout for potential dangers of all sorts.

785 Prepare For Emergencies. The Boy Scout Motto is "Be Prepared." This is certainly true of classrooms and schools when it comes to emergencies such as a bloody nose or a sick child. Plan for possible emergencies *before* they take place.

786 Practice Car Safety. To avoid carjacking, teachers, parents, and students can be taught to:
- Choose well-lighted and busy places to stop for gas or make a phone call.
- Keep the automobile locked and the windows rolled up.
- In a minor accident, signal to the other driver to follow you to the nearest populated area, preferably a police or fire station.

787 Organize Security Parents. To help maintain good student behavior at various school functions, enlist parents of students to serve as "Security Parents." Obtain attractive T-shirts or jackets with "Security Parent" written on them to identify these special helpers. This encourages school safety while it encourages parents to participate in school activities.

SCHEDULES

788 **Flex The Schedule.** Arrange a flex schedule so that senior students who want to work during their senior year may apply for an abbreviated schedule. Students attend school during the morning and work during the afternoon.

789 **Offer College Courses.** Work out a schedule so that qualified students may enroll in selected courses at nearby colleges. Individual schedules for students can be developed with the help of counselors at the school and college.

SCHOOL CLOSING

790

Inviting comes

from courage and

courage comes

from caring.

791 **Transplant The Plants.** In the early spring, students (representing both the new and closing school) can dig up some of the plants from the closing school and plant them in the new school yard. This can be a most significant gesture to "carry the torch" of learning to the new school.

792 **Send A Delegation.** The principal of the new school and a group of his or her faculty and students can travel to the school to be closed and welcome the student body to the new school.

SCHOOL SPIRIT

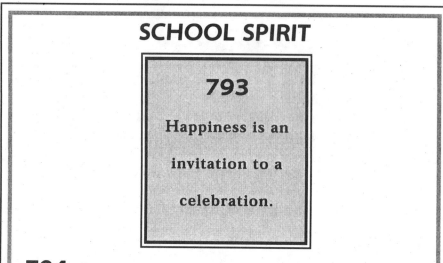

793

Happiness is an

invitation to a

celebration.

794 Buy Some Bumper Stickers. Schools can have bumper stickers made up advertising their school. The parent council or PTA can take on this project and sell the bumper stickers for a profit. This is a very positive way to advertise the school and recognize vehicles from the school's attendance area.

795 Have A School Mascot. A school mascot is a lifesaver when planning programs. The mascot can be the narrator at programs and tie the production together. It can be used as covers for school books, handbooks, on T-shirts, or on sweatshirts. When students know the audience for their composition or work is going to be the school mascot, the quality of the composition or work goes up. Have a costume of the mascot that fits students in the school.

796 Fly The School Colors. Where reasonable, use the school colors in bulletin boards, painted walls, announcements, and even, on special occasions, the dining room food.

797 Order Key Chains. A variety of key chains can be made to inspire parents, students, and teachers. One principal has key chains with a short saying imprinted on one side of the plastic attachment. The saying is "I am proud to be a Lakeside School Teacher." Other key chains that can be made and sold to parents or given as a reward for volunteer work are "I'm proud to be a Radford School Parent" or "Volunteers Keep Vinton School Great."

798 **Choose A Classy Motto.** Allow the class to select a class name, a class motto, a class crest or logo, or class colors to create a more cohesive group. Be sure to encourage new students to participate.

799 **Have A Spirit Day.** The elementary, middle, and high school students can all participate in a spirit day. The students wear school colors, learn school cheers, and meet for a giant all-school pep rally.

800 **Sell Pencils.** Buy five or ten gross of pencils printed with the school name and logo. Offer the pencils for sale in the school store (if one is available) or set a time when the pencils can be purchased at the school office. Make a profit on the pencils and designate the profits to a special school project. Later in the year, give away any unsold pencils as incentives for most improved students.

801 **Give It A Shot.** Periodically provide opportunities where teachers may participate along with students. This may include such "social activities" as basketball free-throw shooting contests, ping pong, or golf. These activities encourage teacher-student social interaction.

802 **Buy A Button Maker.** A button maker is almost a necessity for every school. Making creative buttons is limited only to the imagination of the faculty, staff and students. Selling buttons at carnivals or open houses can also be a money maker. Even though principals are reluctant to spend money on button-making machines, parent councils are often willing to make the investment.

803 **Order Parent T-Shirts.** "I am a Williams School Parent" is a strong way to promote public relations with parents. Educators will be surprised at how many parents will be interested in having a T-shirt, especially if the shirts feature the school logo. All T-shirt sales, both students' and parents', should be pre-paid so that the school is not stuck with dozens of unsold T-shirts.

804 **Hold A Dress Up Day.** Provide a little variety in the school year while promoting school spirit. Have different types of dress up days, Shirt Days, Cap Days, Mismatched Shoe Days, Sweatshirt Days, Special T-Shirt Days, Blue Jean Days, or whatever fits the school area and school colors. One principal who participated in dress up day wore a tuxedo on this special occasion! Students take great pride in their dress regardless of what adults believe.

805 **Cut The Tie.** Educators can wear a special tie to school. Set a special goal such as canned goods for the homeless or other worthwhile student accomplishments. For every ten cans of food contributed, students are allowed to cut off an inch of an educator's tie. Obviously, educators will need a number of old ties to be sacrifice.

SCHOOL STATIONERY

806

Invitational notes

are like

amoxicillin:

It takes a

regular dosage to

kill disinviting

infections.

807 **Sharpen The School Stationery.** School stationery reflects on the entire school. Be sure that it carries the school's address, and telephone *and* FAX numbers. It can also carry the school's mission statement, logo, or motto. One school has a photograph of the entire faculty and staff standing outside the school smiling and waving. This photo is placed across the entire top of the school stationery.

808 **Share School Stationery.** Provide teachers and staff with school stationery to use in their correspondence with parents and professionals. The stationery used by those in the school should be attractive and professional in appearance to communicate a positive message.

SELF-CONCEPT

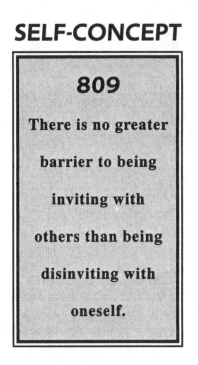

809

There is no greater

barrier to being

inviting with

others than being

disinviting with

oneself.

810 **Make An "I Can."** Cover a small empty fruit-juice can with bright contact paper. Paste a picture of an eye cut from a magazine on the outside of the can. When a student says "I can't" give the student an *I Can*. The *I Can* is good to keep pencils in and to remind the student that "I can!"

SIGNS

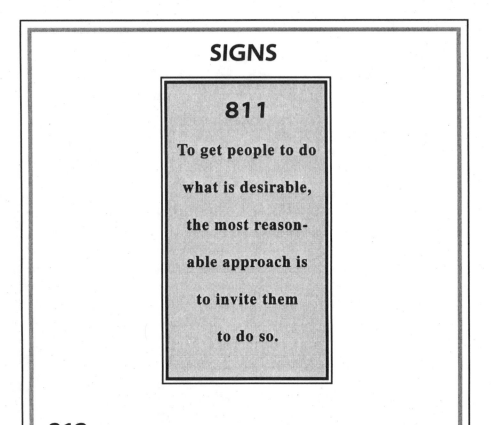

811

To get people to do

what is desirable,

the most reason-

able approach is

to invite them

to do so.

812 Send Window Greetings. Though not to everyone's taste, school window messages, with one letter in each window, can add spirit and enthusiasm to the school. The messages can be a morale booster: "HILLTOP KIDS ARE A-OK," or a cheery greeting: "HAPPY HOLIDAYS." These messages can be accompanied by attractive window displays created by students.

813 Promote Politeness. It is important to insure that every directional sign in and around the school begins with "Please" and ends with "Thank You." Using please and thank you is a good way to improve the atmosphere of the school, to show respect for people, and is an excellent way to accomplish desired goals. "Please walk in hallways. Thank You," works better than "Do not run."

814 **Give Clear Directions.** Signs designed to give directions should be simple, direct and positively worded, to explain to people what TO DO, not what NOT to do. Also, color-coded signs can help to indicate different areas of the building.

815 **Improve Sign Language.** Look carefully at every sign in and around your school. Are they inviting? For example, "Keep Off the Grass," "No Trespassing," "No Parking," "Reserved," "Visitors Must Report...," "Do Not Pick Flowers" can be replaced by "Visitor Parking," "Welcome To Our School," "Please Use Walkways," "Please Leave Flowers For Others To Enjoy." Signs should be as inviting as possible.

816 **Place Some Welcome Decals.** The Midwest Specialities Company (P.O. Box 2026, Kalamazoo, MI 49001) sells decals for glass and solid doors. The decals read "Welcome to our school—Visitors please report to the main office upon entering the building during regular school hours. Thank You." This sign is certainly more professionally inviting than "Visitors Must Report to Office" or "No Trespassing."

817 **Send Electrifying Messages.** Some schools feature an electronic message board in the main foyer of the building. It flashes a welcome greeting to everyone and gives announcements concerning school events. This is particularly helpful in a school that is regularly open for after-school events.

818 **Build A Message Board.** Have volunteers build a large, lighted message board which can be located at the entrance of the school. The board welcomes visitors to the school, offers a greeting, and announces school activities and student achievements.

819 **Create Reader Signs.** Some elementary schools have placed reader signs at their school. Most high schools have something up in front of their schools. Why not a reader sign in front of the elementary school? Things that can be put up on reader signs are: special events, projects, or accomplishments.

This is especially helpful if the school is on a very busy street. It is important to make sure that the board is kept up to date.

820 **Identify The School.** Rather than rely on some small sign on the building or entrance way to identify the school, install some large letters on the building that can be clearly seen from a distance. This shows pride in the school.

821 **Build A Graffiti Outlet.** Want to keep graffiti off the school building? Build students a graffiti wall away from campus or haul in a boulder. Every year the seniors decorate the wall or boulder and it does nothing to detract from the building's neat appearance.

822 **Welcome Everyone.** Make welcome signs for school entrances in various foreign languages. Teachers can help with this, as can students and parents. This is an excellent way to cultivate appreciation for cultural diversity.

823 **Compare Signs.** Every sign in and around schools is inviting or disinviting. Here are some examples:

Inviting Signs:	Disinviting Signs:
Please Use Sidewalks	Office Closed
Welcome	Do Not Disturb
Please Leave Message	Keep Off Grass
Visitor Parking	No Trespassing
Please Use Other Door	No Talking
Open, Come In	No Running In Halls
Thank You For Not Smoking	No Admittance
Come Back Soon	Visitors Must Report...
Open House	No Smoking
We're Glad You're Here	Be Seated
Students Welcome	No Students Allowed

SOCIAL COMMITTEE

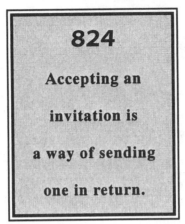

824

Accepting an

invitation is

a way of sending

one in return.

825 Provide Crisis Support. The faculty and staff can prepare meals for a staff member who needs help because of family illness, hospitalization, or a death in the family. Money donations can also be given to help staff members who have incurred unusually large medical bills.

826 Hold "Ice Breaker" Meetings. Organize and carry out a series of meetings (attendance voluntary) where the only goal is to get to know each other on a more personal level. Topics of conversation might be "Who's your Hero and Why?" "What Would Your Perfect School Look Like?" or "What's The Best and Worst Thing About Your Job?" Both faculty and staff are invited to the meetings.

827 Form A Sunshine Committee. The Sunshine Committee collects money in the fall to send flowers or fruit to staff members for various occasions, including weddings, births, retirements, or funerals of an immediate family member. A gift is purchased for the birth of a baby to a staff member. Cards or flowers are sent to others for illness or sympathy.

828 **Create Mysteries.** Arrange to carry out thoughtful acts anonymously for colleagues and students. For example, a drawing for a "secret pal" club, a "Secret Santa" at Christmas, or a "Secret Sweetie" for Valentine's Day, can keep the school spirit alive and provide surprise gifts throughout the school year.

829 **Enhance The Faculty Lounge.** Survey the faculty and staff regarding the faculty lounge. What is wanted? A heavy-duty coffee machine, a no-smoking policy, and hot water for tea are usually appreciated. Fresh flowers provided by the social committee and placed in the teachers' lounge are always a hit.

830 **Organize A Faculty Breakfast.** Several times a year take the time to hold a breakfast, lunch, dinner, or social for sharing and caring. Be sure that new members are involved in the planning. Perhaps a student organization would like to do this to welcome the new year and new staff members. Later in the year, the breakfast could be a celebration of accomplishments.

831 **Find The Ghost Teacher.** Invent a phantom teacher "Ima Blue" or other clever name. "Ima" has her own mailbox, appears on schedules and sends and receives notes to and from faculty, staff, and students. Ima is the special patron spirit of the school.

STORE

832 **Maintain A School-Mart.** A school store is a wonderful way to provide "real-life" experiences for both customers and the student "managers" of the store. A faculty, staff, parent, or community volunteer can supervise the store which can offer school supplies, school spirit items, refreshments, or other special sales. In addition to providing good economic lessons, the store will raise money for school or class projects.

STUDENT GOVERNMENT

833

Leadership is the

ability to dream

great dreams, then

to invite others to

share in them.

834 Honor Student Leaders. Students who fill positions on the student government should receive recognition for their contributions to the school. Their photographs can be placed on bulletin boards, in newsletters, and in the school newspaper. Student leaders should also be properly introduced and recognized during assembly programs.

835 Energize The Student Council. The student government can make real contributions to the school far beyond typical advisory roles. Many schools involve the student councils in policy formulations, fund raisers, and community service projects. The council also can help to plan and coordinate school calendars or sponsor student social events.

836 Organize A Sunshine Committee. Students form a "sunshine committee" to do things for other students. The committee sends cards if a student is in the hospital. The committee also makes attendance phone calls.

STUDENT HELPERS

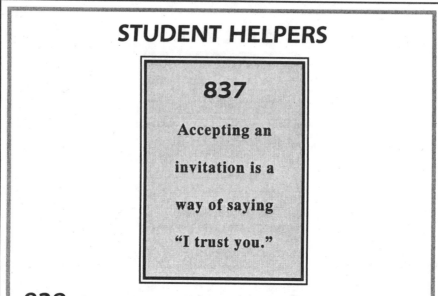

837

Accepting an invitation is a way of saying "I trust you."

838 Organize Peer Helpers. Peer tutoring works great for those students who are having difficulty with certain subjects. Schools which have peer tutoring programs report that students are willing to take time during their lunch hour, and before or after school to work with fellow students.

839 Share Classroom Duties. There are numerous tasks that students can do to help manage the classroom. Taking roll, distributing and collecting materials, preparing experiments, grading papers, and preparing reports are among many tasks that can be used to turn student energy into productive avenues and make life a little easier for the teacher.

840 Arrange A "Big Pal" Program. Tutoring and related activities seem to help both the tutor and the one being tutored. Therefore, arrange a service program in which older students are matched with students from lower grades to offer support, assistance, and friendship.

841 Use Student Aides. Senior students can be invited to serve as student aides. Students can assist in the attendance office, main office, vocational office, guidance office, media center, and school store. Make sure that all aides understand the importance of their professional responsibilities, including the importance of confidentiality.

842 **Organize Student Guides.** Visitors to the school should be met quickly and cordially. Student guides are particularly helpful if the school has many visitors, for they can serve as hosts and hostesses. It sets an inviting tone to have parents, substitutes, and other visitors *escorted* to the place they wish to go and helped with their needs.

843 **Generate Senior Reader Power.** Each semester invite a group of high school seniors to visit an elementary school library and select books they loved as children. The seniors return to high school and practice reading the favorite books aloud with as much animation as possible. The seniors then return to the elementary school, are assigned a class, and read to the elementary students. This could be the beginning of a teaching career.

STUDENT RECOGNITION

844

Human potential, though not always apparent, is always there—waiting to be discovered and invited forth.

845 **Hold Student Recognition Day.** Have a Student Recognition Day at the end of the school year. Insure that every professional in the school has some awards to give. Some ideas for awards are: spelling bee, citizenship, reading 100 books, honor roll, physical fitness, attendance, and essay awards. It is important to announce in the early fall what awards will be given during Student Recognition Day in the spring.

846 **Prepare Some "Tooth Fairy Envelopes."** In elementary schools prepare a special tooth fairy envelope ready for sending home any tooth that comes out at school. A clever little poem signed by the teacher and principal make a special notice of this tender moment in the life of a family.

847 **Recognize Citizens Of The Month.** Each month students can be selected from a number of categories (academic, athletic, extracurricular, leadership, most improved, most considerate, etc.). Their names can be announced over the intercom and their photographs can be placed in the main lobby. Be sure to send letters of congratulations home to parents.

848 **Salute Blue Ribbon Winners.** Rather than the usual certificates, order some blue ribbons with sayings such as "Outstanding Behavior," "Most Improved," "Meritorious School Service," and "Excellent Academic Work."

849 **Give "Good Deed Doer" Cards.** Print "Good Deed Doer" cards with a place for the names of both the teacher and student. Distribute cards to each teacher each week. The teacher completes a card for each student "caught" doing a good deed (holding a door open, picking up paper in the hallway, helping another student) and gives it to the student. The student places it in principal's or counselor's Good Deed Doer Box. Each Monday morning one card is drawn and announced with fanfare during morning P.A. announcements. The winner receives a small prize, perhaps a free lunch.

850 Use Prizes. When student recognition is needed, here are some ideas:

Names announced on P.A.	Refreshments for the entire class
Free time at end of class	Pizza with the principal
Class outside	School T-shirts
Video game vouchers	Meal coupons for hamburgers
Medals, buttons, and pins	Movie tickets
Credit at school store	Positive letter to parents
Certificate from the Principal	Certificate for dinner
Small gifts from local merchants	Video game
Small gifts from PTA	Extra time at computer terminal
Nature walk	Field trip
Classroom video	Gold stars (redeemable)
Puppet shows	School-wide movie

851 Have Lunch At The Captain's Table. Each week a small group of students is selected by a committee to have lunch with the principal. The cafeteria staff can make up trays and serve them at the "Captain's Table." This is a great opportunity for the principal to get to know certain students better in a nonthreatening situation.

852 Name Student Of The Week. Beginning early in the school year, make every student in the room a "Student of the Week." Take a photograph of this student and place it on colorful poster paper in the center of the bulletin board. Invite other students to contribute positive things they have found out about the student. At the end of the week, give the bulletin board material to the student to take home.

853 Be Sensitive With Praise. Not all students are willing or able to accept praise, particularly praise given to them in front of their friends. A private comment to let a student know how pleased the teacher is with his or her behavior might be more appropriate.

854 **Send Double-Strength Compliments.** As nice as it is to receive kind words directly, it's even nicer to learn that kind words about oneself have been expressed to others. Rather than praising a student directly, praising the student to teachers, parents, or other students can be highly effective. The original praise will reach the person with double impact!

855 **Spread Positive Rumors.** Take note of something positive a student does, then describe it to the class without mentioning the student's name. The purpose of positive rumors is to let students know how good they are and how much they can learn. When a teacher remarks, "I noticed how courteous a certain student was this morning," it compliments the entire class.

856 **Spotlight A Special Student.** Arrange things so that a less-popular student can earn the right for the entire class to receive some special treat, such as a movie, a refreshment, or free time. This less-popular student will be enhanced in the eyes of classmates.

857 **Give Gold Credit Cards.** Students achieving Honor Roll status (3.0 G.P.A. or better) receive a Gold Credit Card. This card entitles the holder free admission to all events, discounts in the school store, and unlimited use of the Media Center with teacher's permission.

858 **Send Them To The Principal.** Put together a certificate that says "Sent to the Principal." When teachers send a student to the principal for something good, an extra effort, or to share a good idea, the principal in return fills out a short note congratulating them. The teacher signs it and the students take it home. It is a way to accentuate the positive in the school.

859 **Write "I Notices."** Report cards of all those who made the honor roll are shared with the principal. The principal writes a brief personal note of praise for those good grades. Students are always pleased at the personal recognition, and parents soon spread the word that the principal took the time to write on their child's report card.

860 **Be Principal For A Day.** Set up a "Principal for a Day" program in your school. Create an incentive that will have children earn the right to be principal for a day. This can be monthly, quarterly, or yearly. It can be structured around a reading program, a behavioral program, or any other criteria that you set up. After the student or students have been selected, let them follow you around for a day and help you make decisions. Structure the day so that they will make some of the school's decisions. It will be one of those unusual treats in their school career. And they will not forget it.

STUDENT-TEACHER INTERNS

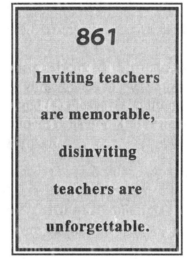

861

Inviting teachers

are memorable,

disinviting

teachers are

unforgettable.

862 **Write A Survival Manual.** Develop a simple procedure manual to provide student interns with information about the school. State school rules in positive terms, letting the student teacher know what to do, not what not to do. Good communication about policies assures good understanding and likely enforcement.

863 **Mentor Student-Teacher Interns.** In addition to the teacher who is working most closely with the student-teacher intern, encourage other teachers to provide mentoring. Mentoring may include eating lunch with the student, discussing ideas about teaching in the faculty lounge, or providing information about the school.

SUBSTITUTES

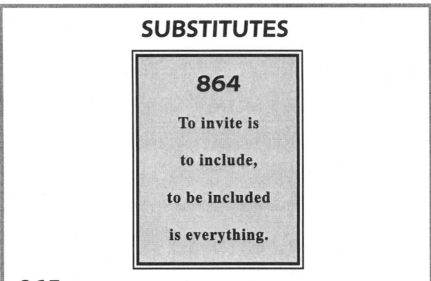

864

To invite is

to include,

to be included

is everything.

865 Form A Substitute Buddy System. Assign an informal "advisor" to each substitute to help him or her with school procedures, answer questions, have lunch, and provide assistance as needed throughout the day. This will let substitutes know that their work is appreciated.

866 Prepare A Substitute Care Package. Prepare a packet of information for each substitute that includes the school code of conduct and a clear map of the building with directions for restrooms and the cafeteria. Make a list of names of teachers in nearby rooms, as well as counselors and principal, and a contact person in case of an emergencies. The packet can provide suggestions for what to do in case there is no lesson plan available; for example, some generic lessons, readings or puzzles.

867 Provide Backup. Being a substitute teacher can be threatening (perhaps a strange school, classroom, student). Each substitute should be visited at least once each day by an administrator to demonstrate support.

868 Remember The Sub. It is important to include substitute teachers in all educational activities. This includes opening-of-school meetings (with special introductions), districtwide meetings, regular faculty meetings, and all social events. For substitutes to do a good job in the school, they need to feel a part of the school family.

869 Organize Super Subs. Suggest that central office personnel volunteer one day each year to be a substitute teacher. This keeps the central office in contact with the day-to-day challenges faced by classroom teachers and is a wonderful morale booster for teachers.

870 Spotlight The Substitute. When a new substitute checks in at the office, use a polaroid to take a photograph and place the photograph along with his or her name in the teachers' workroom. It allows teachers to put a name and a face together and makes the substitute feel welcome.

871 Support The Substitute. Substitute teachers are a vital part of any school. To help them in their sometimes difficult task, provide a training program, assign a "buddy" teacher to help them in time of need, and develop a manual of helpful do's and don'ts that is given to everyone on the substitute list.

872 Bring On The Subs. For special professional training programs, try to avoid programs on "tired time" (after school meetings) by hiring subs to release teachers and staff for special training. This greatly enriches the quality of the training *and* the morale of the faculty and staff.

SUGGESTION BOX

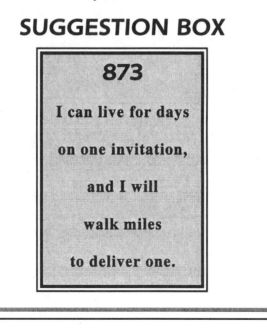

873

I can live for days

on one invitation,

and I will

walk miles

to deliver one.

874 **Capture Ideas.** A suggestion box to encourage input is made available to everyone in and around the school, including families. The suggestion box can be mounted in a hallway, and the suggestions that come from these boxes can be signed or unsigned. Many schools find that the idea box can offer some valuable suggestions for improving many aspects of the school.

875 **Elicit Suggestions.** Organize a suggestion box in the faculty lounge or workroom to ask faculty and staff for suggestions about how they can improve their school.

SUMMER ACTIVITIES

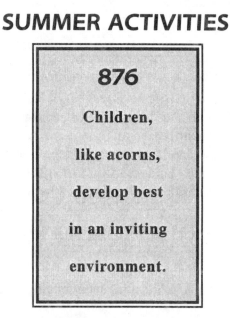

876

Children,

like acorns,

develop best

in an inviting

environment.

877 **Maintain A Model Class-room.** Classrooms are usually "stripped" of all decorations during the summer to allow workers to clean and paint. Summer is often the time when new students and parents visit the school, so suggest that the classroom closest to the office be beautifully decorated all during summer. The principal can take incoming students and parents to this room to show them how inviting the school will be come fall.

878 **Encourage Summer Reading.** Find ways to get students to read during the summer months. Successful summer reading programs have taken many forms, including "Love of Reading" projects with assigned books, required readings identified by the next grade teacher (or English Department), or finding ways to open the school library periodically during the summertime.

SUPPORT STAFF

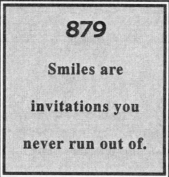

879

Smiles are

invitations you

never run out of.

880 **Hold An Appreciation Day.** Hold an appreciation day for all support staff, including bus drivers, custodians, cafeteria workers, secretaries, paraprofessionals and other non-instructional staff members. Show them how much they are appreciated by having a brunch or lunch, presenting them with small gifts, and giving each a letter of thanks.

881 **Schedule An Aide Meeting.** Most schools have a number of aides on the staff. Meet with them periodically to show them that they are important. Even if there is no agenda, bring them together, serve refreshments, and ask them what they would like to discuss. It makes them feel that their job is vital to the operation of the school.

882 **Award The "Golden Trash Can."** Obtain an ordinary classroom trash can and spray paint it gold. At the end of each week the custodians select the cleanest classroom for that week. That class gets to keep the Golden Trash Can until next week's winner is chosen. At the end of the year the classroom that won the

Golden Trash Can the most times gets to keep the can permanently. This simple incentive makes the custodial staff feel a part of the school while encouraging everyone to keep the school clean.

883 **Post Some Photographs.** Arrange to have framed photographs of secretaries, food-service professionals, custodians, and other support staff mounted along with their names. This recognizes their major contributions to the school.

TEACHING TECHNIQUES

884

All the good

intentions in

the world will not

add up to a

single inviting act.

885 **Warm Up The Class.** At the beginning of each class period a personal greeting, a little light humor, a brief comment on world events, or an inquiry into how things are going can set the stage for learning. Just as joggers should limber up their muscles before jogging, teachers should limber up their classes before teaching.

886 **Laugh A Little.** Classrooms can be hilarious places. Teachers and students often say funny things they don't intend to say or notice humor in something being studied. Laughter warms a classroom. Teachers and students who "goof something up" in the classroom can share their humanness by laughing at the situation.

887 **Be The Greeter.** At the beginning and end of each class session, take a minute or two to establish a caring environment. Share a thought, talk about a current event, or ask about students' concerns. Let students know that everyone is a human being first, and a teacher or student second.

888 **Use Inclusive Pronouns.** Using such pronouns as *we, us,* and *our* is much more likely to create a positive classroom environment than using *you, mine,* and *yours.* For example, saying, "We need to finish our work on time" is preferable to "You students must complete your work." Using the collective term promotes community and shared responsibility.

889 **Ask For The Order.** There is a skill in asking for what is wanted without demanding it. Like any skill, it takes practice to ask again (and again) without ordering or commanding. Make your request in simple and specific terms rather than hinting. The more explicit an invitation, the more likely it will be received and accepted.

890 **Talk Facing The Class.** Remember that in some mainstreamed classes lip readers must be able to see the teacher's face. Avoid the habit of talking towards the black board or overhead projector screen.

891 **Promote Collections.** Almost every student has collected something—soft drink cans, rocks, baseball cards, music boxes, dolls, matchbox covers. Collecting can lead to all sorts of marvelous learning and future careers. Encourage students to begin collections. If they already have a collection, invite them to display it in the school. Studies of geniuses have found that they almost all share the universal characteristic of collecting things.

892 **Collect Junk.** While looking for books at flea markets and garage sales, also look for objects that can be taken apart, put back together, and manipulated (i.e., broken typewriters, clocks, and simple mechanical devices). Puzzles, toys, and gadgets can all be used to encourage imagination, develop simulation games, and invite learning. These activities have the potential to encourage learning while inviting positive changes in self-concept.

893 **Maintain A Costume Closet.** Old hats, uniforms, costumes, masks, and unusual clothing can be used for class plays, role-playing activities, self-directed dramatizations, and related activities. Such activities are particularly successful in the teaching of reading. Yard sales are a great source of supplies.

894 **Be With It.** Make an effort to understand the world of today's student. For example, try to keep up with fads, fashions, popular heroes, latest films, sports, T.V. programs, actors, singers, and other current interests of students. Using an instance from a current T.V. program to invite learning of an academic concept can be quite effective.

895 **Handling The Unacceptable.** When a student has submitted something unacceptable, try this approach: "I think you can do better than this." Point out ways the work can be improved, then say: "I want you to try again." This encourages both student responsibility and academic success.

896 **Tap Expertise.** The school food-service professional may be a "bug" on classical music, the bus driver an amateur artist, or the school psychologist or nurse a rock collector. The principal may be a woodworker and a fellow teacher a ballet dancer. Find the talents of people in school and invite them to share their interests and lives with students.

897 **Hold A Contest.** For a few minutes at the beginning or end of a class session, hold a contest to loosen things up. For example, a contest for the "most terrible pun" or "most trivial trivia" can invite a warm and friendly class feeling.

898 **Send Unconditional Invitations.** Send invitations that suggest acceptance, not rejection. For example, saying, "I think you can do this work, so practice" is much more positive than saying: "I think you can *if* you will try." Unconditional statements of support carry weight.

899 Put The "Can't" Out. Cut silhouettes of black cats out of construction paper. When some student says "I can't," go to a door, open it, and gently place the "can't" in the hallway. It's a way of reminding the students that "can't never could do anything."

900 Be Mature. When children act like children, adults should act like adults. The most mature person can change his or her behavior easiest. Who is the most mature person in the classroom?

901 Hold The Point. Champion bird dogs are judged in part by how long they "hold the point" when they detect a covey of birds. It's been reported that a champion bird dog becomes so committed to pointing birds that when it is "at point" the dog can be lifted completely off the ground and it will not break its point! Similarly, champion educators are judged by the consistent and dependable way in which they function.

902 Increase Wait-Time. Increase "wait-time" (length of pause) when waiting for nonassertive students to respond to questions. This will encourage the student to feel worthwhile and capable.

903 Assign "Insight Cards." Have schedule cards turned in by students at regular intervals. These "insight" cards can provide a regular vehicle for students to voice concerns, offer suggestions, or share observations. It is an excellent form of classroom communication, particularly with shy or reserved students who are slow to speak out in class.

904 Try A Four-Day Work Week. Encouraging students to complete the class work schedule in four days, rather than the usual five, can open Fridays for special activities. This arrangement serves as a powerful incentive to finish the required work as quickly as possible.

905 Fight Boredom. The cardinal sin of teaching is to bore people to death. Consider boredom the number one enemy in the classroom. Devise games, contests, exercises, demonstrations, presentations. competitions and challenges to fight boredom. And remember the adage: "If you are bored, it's because you are boring."

906 Take A Sound Walk. On a comfortable day, take the students outdoors for a sound walk. Ask students to take a paper, sit in a quiet place, and list all the sounds they hear from "Mother Nature." Also, ask them to list all the sounds they hear made by humans and their inventions. Later, form small groups of students and ask them to share their perceptions.

907 Encourage All Students In Physical Education. When there are nonparticipants in physical education classes, find something for them to do besides sitting in the bleachers and watching. For example, ask them to serve as line judges, spotters, or scorekeepers.

908 Be Creative In Physical Education Classes. Ask skilled athletes to use only one hand, or reverse the hand with which they usually perform. This allows even skilled athletes to develop further.

909 Use Positive Language. Sometimes students are intimidated by language used in physical education or sports, especially those who do not perceive themselves as athletic. Avoiding terms such as "suicides," "crunchers," or "drill murder" may encourage some students to perceive exercise and athletics as activities which they can master.

TEAMING

> ## 910
>
> Invitations come
>
> in all sizes—
>
> small (smile);
>
> medium (share a
>
> meal); and large
>
> (share a lifetime).

911 Create Interdisciplinary Teaming. Working to create team planning time (i.e., coordination of instruction involving several curriculum areas, scheduling tests and projects, and planning lessons) is very important. Remember to include "special" teachers in team meetings.

912 Insure Success With Teams. Often academic teams fail because there is a lack of understanding regarding procedures and expectations. To avoid failure and encourage success with teams, practice the "Three D's":

Define a clear mission for the teams.

Determine the role of team members.

Develop team-building rituals and team spirit.

TELEPHONES

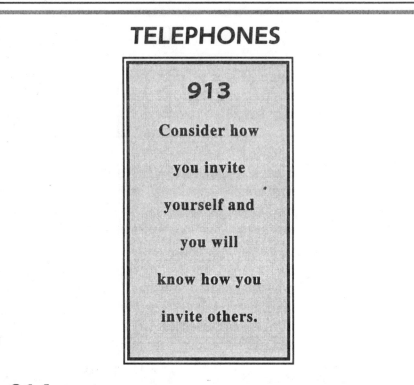

913

Consider how

you invite

yourself and

you will

know how you

invite others.

914 **Arrange A Little Privacy.** There are times when a faculty member needs privacy for a phone call. A school phone should be made available for this purpose, with a 25 cent charge for personal calls.

915 **Call-A-Week.** Many teachers have taken the time to make one phone call per week to a parent, not including regular conferences. Many principals are taking this one step farther and making a minimum of one phone call per week to the family of someone who is caught doing something good. This can be about something that the principal sees or something that a teacher suggests. It is an outstanding school/family outreach and develops a positive relationship between home and school.

916 **Thank The Caller.** When a caller must be transferred or placed on hold, express appreciation for the caller's patience. And be sure to see that someone stays with the call until the transfer is completed.

917 **View The Telephone As An Ally.** Most communication with schools is by telephone. Are callers greeted promptly, courteously, and pleasantly when they call the school? When answering the telephone, make the caller feel welcome by using three steps: (1) *Welcome:* "Good Morning," (2) *Identification*: "Jefferson High School," and (3) *Offer to assist:* "May I help you?" Convey the message that the caller is important. (Remember, a smile can be heard over the phone).

918 **Hold Those Calls.** When an educator is with a visitor, it is a most inviting act for the executive to say to his or her secretary: "Will you please hold incoming calls for the next ten minutes?" This is an indirect way of saying to the visitor, "You are important, and for the next ten minutes, I do not want us to be interrupted." This lets the visitor know that he or she is important. It also sets some time constraints.

919 **Install A Student Telephone.** Providing a centrally located telephone that does not require permission to use is a special way to invite students to see themselves as able, valuable, and responsible. The phone can be programmed to take only local calls. Installing a student phone is worth the relatively small cost, for it reflects respect for students. When students are treated with respect, they are more likely to *show* respect.

920 **Share A Phone.** School telephones are sometimes protected as though they were a symbol of power. In many schools, teachers and other professionals do not have access to a "private" phone, and yet often need one. By making a phone available to others during appropriate times, the school demonstrates an effort to develop a cooperative and caring relationship with everyone.

921 Phone With Concern. When a student misses school, call the home that morning and find out how the student is doing. Tell students they're missed. Keep phoning until attendance improves. A follow-up phone call to parents or guardians during evening hours may be necessary to check on the welfare of the student.

922 Take Accurate Messages. Always take time to write clear, unmistakable phone messages. Include name of caller, the caller's number (including area code), date, time, and the message (if any). *Repeat* the message to confirm its accuracy to the sender's satisfaction.

923 Use The 30/30 Technique. Answer the phone in three rings or fewer. Recognize any person entering the school office in thirty seconds or less.

924 Send A Special Invitation. Make personal phone calls to all parents of students who will be receiving awards at assemblies and ask them to attend. Many family members do not realize how much it means to their children for them to be present.

925 Install A Telephone. A telephone *in every classroom in the school* would encourage professionalism, promote safety in emergencies, and be a great morale booster to the teacher. The phones can be programmed for local calls only. The idea is worth exploring with the local telephone company. Remember to ask for a special discount. Most businesses want to support education.

926 Take It Standing Up. Whenever it is necessary to make or take an important phone call, always stand up. When a person is standing, the voice is stronger and the body is in an assertive position. The call will be much easier to handle standing up.

927 **Identify Yourself.** When answering the telephone it helps to identify yourself to the caller. One might say, "Good morning, Smith High School, Ellie Smith speaking. May I help you?"

928 **Return Messages.** Check for telephone messages often and return them as soon as possible. Promptness in returning telephone calls helps create a positive perception of the school and how it functions.

929 **Leave Word.** When you leave the school during the day, let the secretary know where you have gone and when you expect to return. This courtesy makes it possible for the secretary or receptionist to communicate more accurately with a caller.

930 **Create A Call List.** Keep a list of numbers of people you call often. These may be school officials, parent volunteers, or staff with whom you work.

931 **Transfer Calls Sparingly.** When possible, avoid transferring a call. If you can, help a caller by providing information. It speeds up the communication process.

932 **Use Professional Language.** Realize that when you are on the phone you are the "Voice of the School." *Always* be courteous and professional. Avoid using slang or technical terms when communicating with others. Be natural and use language that communicates your message clearly.

933 **Be Pleasant.** Smiles can be "heard" over the telephone, as can impatient attitudes. Show by your voice that you are interested in being helpful. Use the caller's name to add a personal touch.

934 **Treat Every Call As Important.** No matter the reason for the call, treat each caller with respect and thank him or her for calling. No phone call should be treated as insignificant.

935 **Don't Leave Caller Hanging.** If a caller decides to stay on the line, use the "hold" button. If the telephone does not have a "hold" button, lay the handset down quietly. Communicate with the caller every thirty seconds to assure him or her that you are aware that the caller is still holding.

936 **Use Discretion.** When someone cannot be reached by phone, tell the caller that "the person is not available just now. May I take a message?" This is more appropriate than saying that the person is on a coffee break or in the bathroom.

937 **Develop Guidelines For Calls.** If you are handling incoming calls, find out from the administrator what kinds of calls he or she will accept even when in an important meeting or somewhere else in the building.

938 **Be Clear About Questions From The Press.** Find out from your administrator what kind of questions from the press you might answer and the type of questions he or she would prefer to deal with directly. This is particularly important to do before crisis situations occur.

939 **Establish Guidelines For Emergencies.** Establish guidelines for handling calls during an emergency, such as a storm or bomb threat.

TEXTBOOKS

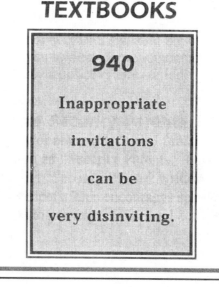

940

Inappropriate

invitations

can be

very disinviting.

941 **Involve Students In Selection.** If the school system is one in which teachers select textbooks, ask students of varying backgrounds and achievement to help preview the books before decisions are made. After all, who knows better than students which books are inviting? (Students can also participate in the decision-making process in other areas, such as rules of conduct, academic expectations, and teacher selection!)

TIME MANAGEMENT

942

You may be

inviting too

early, but that

is better than

being inviting

too late.

943 **Practice The Rule Of Four.** It is important to trust people to do an adequate job. The rule of four states that the educator is usually wasting valuable energy when he or she is doing work that a student or volunteer could do just as well with four hours of training or less. If the educator tries to do everything in the classroom, he or she will also have to do it next time, since no one else has learned how.

944 Arrange Free-Time Options. Post and explain free-time options so that students know what they can do when they finish their work early. These options can include a good book selection, filmstrip projectors, or videotapes. Quick finishers will rarely have reason to misbehave or to claim "I'm bored."

945 Get There Early. There are countless causes of tension and anxiety that are unavoidable. Yet one major cause of tension that can easily be avoided is cutting time too short and running behind. Make a vow to set the alarm clock a little earlier and arrive at the school cool, calm, and collected. Arriving early for any activity can reduce a lot of self-inflicted anxiety.

946 Hang A Wall Clock. For offices, place a small clock behind where guests are seated. This way time schedules can be maintained without consulting one's wrist watch, which can be viewed by guests as a "disinviting" act.

947 Budget Time. Develop a system (a checklist of "things to do" or a schedule of important events to attend) and manage available time accordingly. Budgeting time helps you expend energy evenly so that no one area or task consumes too much attention.

948 Check Timing. Timing is very important in the inviting process. Too much, too soon, too little, too late can weaken the best invitation. Educators should ask themselves: *What* invitation, by *whom,* is most likely to be accepted by *this* person at *this* time?

949 Be A Clock Watcher. A small clock somewhere in easy view will help start and end classes on time and use class time efficiently. Promptness on the teacher's part establishes an "on time—on task—no-nonsense" class climate.

950 Rethink The School Schedule. Arrange the school schedule so that teachers who are working together on interdisciplinary teams or projects have the same preparation and lunch periods.

951 **Use School Time.** Plan time outside the classroom during the school day to focus on school improvement. It is unlikely that planning done on the fringes of the school day will become a major part of the school. Ways to provide time for small teams to accomplish this might include the use of administrative personnel as substitutes, along with cooperative arrangements with colleges and universities.

952 **Heal Misunderstandings Promptly.** Work to insure that yesterday's misunderstandings do not interfere with today's opportunities. Seek to clear up misunderstandings quickly.

953 **Practice Quick Response Time.** When someone (student, teacher, parents, or community member) contacts the school regarding a concern, practice quick response time. Ideally, a response should be within one day.

954 **Give Lead Time.** Whenever possible, allow adequate time for meeting deadlines. The administrator should be able and willing to talk with staff about the energy, materials, and time needed to insure completion of tasks on schedule.

955 **Take Advantage Of Time.** Every educator knows the frustration of seeing students with problems from home over which the school has little or no control. But educators do have a few precious minutes each day to reach and teach each student. Take advantage of these and don't waste a minute. For some students, these few moments can be an oasis in the desert.

956 **Allow Adequate Time.** Allow adequate time for meeting deadlines. Everyone involved should be able to discuss human resources, materials, and time needed to insure completion of a task. In most cases where the stress level is high, performance is low.

957 Do It Now. Some concerns can be handled right at the moment, rather than later. Picking up the telephone, or dictating a letter to address the concern of a person who is with you at the moment, can be a most inviting act. It is far more effective than stating: "I'll get back to you on this."

958 Offer A Limited Time Invitation. To extend an invitation that is most likely to be accepted, offer a "limited time" invitation. For example, "I have only ten minutes before I must attend a meeting, but meanwhile let's have a cup of coffee and talk." This limits the amount of time the educator is investing.

U.S. MAIL

959 Maintain A Mailbox. A real mailbox located somewhere in the elementary classroom enables students to send notes to each other and to the teacher. Invite students to use the mailbox as a vehicle for suggesting discussion topics. Also, the teacher can use the mailbox to communicate positive messages to students. (To insure that some students are not overlooked, the teacher can keep a private roster of student names to check off as notes are sent and received).

960 Send Mail To The School Board. Place the names and addresses of all school board members on the school's mailing list. Send them copies of all newsletters, handbooks, yearbooks, and the like. Include in the mailings an open invitation to visit the school and see the results of various projects.

961 Organize A Post Card Express. The school supplies post cards with stamps for each teacher. Teachers are asked to send "good news post cards" home regularly identifying children's successes with the curriculum. This is particularly useful for "at-risk" students.

962 Send Parent Congratulatory Letters.
Everyone likes to get recognition. Occasionally, family members make the paper for an outstanding achievement, award, or recognition. Take time to drop them a congratulatory note. This will also give students pride in their family's accomplishment. It is another good way to link school and home.

963 Write "Get Well Quick" Notes. A letter from the school to the student who is going to be away from school for a prolonged period is the best medicine a child can get. The message need be nothing more than a sheet of school stationery containing a cheery note and signed by classmates and faculty. (A photograph of everyone standing outside the school waving makes a *great* letterhead for school stationery.)

964 Send "Proud Principal" Cards. These are post cards mailed to parents from the principal commending a child's academic excellence or improvement. Positive classroom contributions are also recognized.

VIDEO

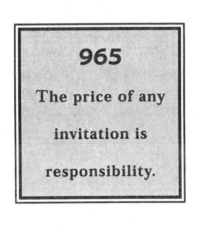

965

The price of any

invitation is

responsibility.

966 **Produce A School Video Special.** This video-tape can be used for many purposes. Uses include showing the tape to parents and other visitors to the school, using it for orientation, mailing a copy to families who are considering relocation, and organizing a video exchange with schools in other parts of the country.

967 **Train Video Specialists.** Train two upper grade students to be school video specialists. These students will do all the videotaping during programs and special events. Surprisingly, students will take more interest in taping than a parent or teacher. Giving an award to the video specialists at the end of the year is essential.

968 **Video Grades.** Create a videotape for each grade level in the school. All plays, special performances, or special activities are recorded with video camera. This tape then follows the students as they go through school. By the end of seven years, all the students' performances are on tape. This makes an excellent exit video for parents and students at the end of the last grade.

969 **Check Out Some Videos.** Take videos of various school events. Obtain support from video store managers to have these tapes available in the stores for parents and members of the community who could not make it to the event itself.

VIOLENCE

970 **Organize "Parent Patrol" Teams.** These teams of volunteer parents provide adult role models, increase the safety of the school, and encourage parent involvement in what happens in and around schools. Attractive T-shirts or school jackets embossed with "Parent Patrol" add to the visibility of the patrols at athletic events, school programs, hallway monitoring, and other functions. It is important that these parents receive proper training and an orientation as to their exact role. It is also vital that they be properly recognized for their efforts at school assemblies and other activities.

971 **Be Consistently Respectful.** Consistently respectful treatment is required to keep small challenges from becoming violent confrontations. Spend time in finding a remedy to the immediate concern rather than trying to find fault.

972 **Teach Conflict Management.** Everyone in the school, including faculty, staff, students, and volunteers should receive comprehensive training in stress and conflict management. Parent education programs that provide training for families can also be introduced at various school functions and special classes.

973 **Know The Trouble Spots.** Back hallways and stairwells, out of the way corners, restrooms, and entrances and exits to schools are often the most likely places for violence to occur. Educators should be highly visible in those areas.

974 **Look Before Leaping.** Try to empathize before making a quick decision. Sometimes common sense becomes an uncommon commodity. Anyone can go from persuasion to confrontation, but it is difficult to go the other way.

975 **Encourage Students To Dress Down.** Stealing is a major concern in many schools. Theft of a student's expensive cap, jacket, or shoes can quickly escalate into an ugly confrontation, with possible deadly results. Warn parents of the dangers of sending their children to school with expensive clothing, jewelry, or possessions. Rules for appropriate dress should be clearly stated.

976 **Stamp Out Rumors Immediately.** Rumors spring up when reliable information is lacking, and have the potential to ignite violent reactions. The best way to combat rumors is to provide continual and accurate information. Bulletin boards, newspapers and newsletters, television and radio, telephone hot lines, public address systems, and school assemblies can all be used to provide information and stamp out rumors.

977 Organize A Crisis Team. This team of students, parents, faculty, and staff is given specific training in crisis management to deal with the inevitable emergency events that occur. These crisis events may be natural or societal. It is essential that the school have a quick response crisis team in position. School counselors are usually the ideal choice to organize and direct these teams.

978 Look For Causes. Sometimes the causes of violence in schools lie with systems rather with people. For example, running in the halls, pushing and shoving, may be caused by buses leaving school within minutes of the end of the school day. Changing policies may eliminate some causes of violence.

979 Conduct Group Guidance Activities. Group guidance activities that emphasize prevention of problems can promote personal responsibility and self-understanding among students and others.

980 Organize Peer Mediation Teams. Helping students learn how to take responsibility and resolve disagreements through peer mediation is beneficial. Students could elect those they believe should become peer mediators for a specific school year. This team of peer mediators could then be trained to work together to resolve difficulties. Disruptive students could then have the choice of either staff interventions or requesting a session with the mediation team.

981 Assume Leadership Qualities. The best way to be a leader in the school is to act like one. It is possible to be an authority in the school without becoming authoritarian. A calm, reasonable, poised action will go a long way in preventing violence in the school.

982 **Insure Success For ALL Students.** Find as many ways as possible to insure that all students have a reasonable chance of success in all school activities, both academic and nonacademic. This includes participating on homecoming courts, athletic teams, cheerleading squads and clubs, as well as academically oriented groups. Providing school success for only a select few is a breeding ground for school violence.

983 **Sponsor "Alumni" Activities.** Having successful alumni return to their alma mater (elementary, middle, or high school) demonstrates that students can achieve their goals and aspirations. Often when such alumni are encouraged to participate in school activities, they encourage increased community support for schools and students.

984 **Celebrate Cultural Diversity.** What better way to learn about other cultures than by celebrating holidays from around the world. Many students within classrooms have a wealth of knowledge related to other cultures. Often, they are eager to share experiences. Such celebrations can emphasize the value and richness of diversity and amplify the commonalities within humankind.

985 **Student Mentoring.** Students helping students promotes an atmosphere of encouragement. Younger students tend to emulate older students. Older students can help acculturate younger students to new buildings and new rules. Older students can help younger students with specific school projects or homework assignments. Such relationships are helpful in at least three ways. First, younger students receive individual attention and encouragement. This suggests that they are important. Second, they suggest that another person is interested in their progress. Finally, older students learn that their behaviors and actions have a significant effect upon younger students. This in turn encourages a sense of responsibility and pride.

VISITORS

987 **Provide Special Space.** Be sure the school has space available for visitors to wait or for parents to meet with teachers. These areas need to be comfortable and decorated to produce an inviting atmosphere. After the meeting, follow things up with a personal "thank you" note for visiting the school.

988 **Show Guests A Videotape.** An attractive videotape that introduces the school can be made available for viewing while visitors are waiting for the arrival of some particular person in the school. This brief tape might be prepared by students.

989 **Offer Refreshments To Visitors.** Breaking bread together is an ancient sign of peace and friendship. By offering each guest coffee, tea, or light refreshment, the stage is set for the resolution of concerns and facilitation of good feelings.

990 **Roll Out The Red Carpet.** Have guests met quickly and cordially. Student guides who serve as host or hostess are particularly helpful. Too often, visitors, new students, and substitutes are left to fend for themselves. A statement such as, "Go to the gym and pick up your key, then report to Mrs. Smith to fill out Form 2109D" without any explanation of how to get there, can be confusing. It sets a special inviting tone to have parents, visitors, and others *escorted* to the place they need to be and *helped* with their concerns.

991 **Identify The Staff.** Purchase attractive name plates for each secretary and other office professionals' desks. This encourages professional politeness and is a great help to the visitor.

992 **Reserve Parking For Guests.** Select several parking spots near the front entrance to the school and place attractive signs marked "Visitor Parking." It sets a nice tone for the guest even before he or she enters the school.

VOLUNTEERS

993

In inviting schools,

as in inviting

families, the

pronouns "us" and

"we" are used

more frequently

than "I" and "you".

994 **Tap Parent Power.** Many school programs use parents or other volunteers as resources. Volunteers can fill many roles, including tutoring, typing, filing, monitoring, grading, storytelling, chaperoning, working on special projects, and even teaching mini-courses on special occupations or skills. Most communities have volunteers available.

995 **Send Parents Questionnaires.** In the fall, send parents a checklist of school projects and activities with which the school could use help. Also, ask if parents have a talent or skill they are willing to share. Duplicate the checklist so that one copy goes to the teacher, one copy to the room parent, and one to the parent volunteer coordinator. Be sure to *use* parents who volunteer.

996 **Give "Super Volunteer" Buttons.** Many schools give special recognition to volunteers by presenting them with "Super Volunteer" buttons. This gives them a special feeling of being appreciated for their work on behalf of students.

997 **Use Room Parent Power.** Most elementary school teachers have a room parent who assists them during special party times. An offshoot of this is to have a room parent to use for projects other than parties. A room parent does not do all the work, but contacts other parents when help is needed. Suggestions for projects include listening to children read, helping with bulletin boards, and assisting with special school projects such as open houses or fairs. A room parent can be an asset to any academic program.

998 **Arrange A "Big Pal" Program.** Tutoring and related activities seem to help both the tutor and the tutored. Therefore, arrange a program where advanced students (or college students) are matched with students from lower grades to offer support, assistance, and friendship. Everyone benefits!

999 **Use Senior Citizen Helpers.** There are many senior citizens who are very capable and would love to come into schools to help. Check with local church and synagogue groups from various ethnic communities in the area. Senior citizens make great listening friends, library helpers, or general volunteers. When asking people to volunteer, explain how much time is required. People are more likely to volunteer when they know the time commitment beforehand.

1000 **Set Up A Ph.D. Program—Parents Help and Dedication.** Set up a Ph.D. program in the school. At the end of the school year, during an awards assembly, give out Ph.D degrees to school volunteers. Use imagination to come up with some special type of certificate. Parents treasure the certificates they get from their child's school.

1001 **Volunteer Luncheon.** At the end of each year, the principal invites all parent workers and helpers to a special brunch, luncheon, or dinner. This can be done by having a potluck or working with an outside catering service. Most school districts will assist in the expense of putting on such an event. Celebrate accomplishments of the volunteers, and invite teachers. Certificates can be given. Thanking parents in a special way will assist in recruiting parent volunteers for the following year. Have a musical group from school provide entertainment.

1002 **Hitch A Ride.** Recruit volunteer parents to drive students who would like to participate in a certain activity but need transportation.

1003 **Train The Volunteers.** Give all volunteers adequate training. Let them observe someone doing what they are expected to do, and be sure to provide adequate information and supervision.

1004 **Hold Volunteer Meetings.** It is important to give volunteers the opportunity to meet together to share concerns and experiences. This provides an informal support group for newcomers to the volunteer team.

1005 Offer Reciprocal Evaluation. Volunteers need, want, and appreciate feedback. Most also have good suggestions for improving the job they are doing. Give volunteers the opportunity to share their evaluations of what's working in the school and what could be done better.

WELLNESS

1006

Invite! Ignite!

Excite! If not

today, do it

tonight!

1007 Organize A Wellness Program. Creating a wellness program in the school can move everyone toward good health. The program is voluntary and includes a walking program, aerobics after school, health checks, and a jogging club. Commitment to staying in shape can become as much a habit as brushing one's teeth.

1008 Make The Gym Available. Arrange for the gym to be open early mornings or evenings for various exercise activities. These activities can include use of exercise equipment and can involve parents as volunteer gym managers.

1009 Play That Funky Music. Use music to add tempo to warm-up exercises in physical education. Let students bring in their favorite records to provide the beat while they exercise. This adds a new and exciting dimension to exercising and can help make an otherwise boring activity exciting and fun.

1010 Call The Doctor. Many physicians and dentists in an attendance area or community are willing to talk with students about good health and will examine teeth on a quick screening basis. In addition, community doctors can be used as health speakers and give talks on the delicate but vitally important subject of sex education. Medical doctors carry weight with students.

1011 Hold A Health Fair. All students, faculty, and staff participate in a schoolwide Health Fair. The Health Department can offer a wide variety of health activities and displays in which everyone may participate.

1012 Create A Smoke-Free School. While it is an inconvenience for some faculty and staff, eliminating cigarettes and other potentially injurious substances makes good sense for everyone. This means eliminating ashtrays in office workshops and lounge areas and adding "This is a smoke-free environment: Thank you for not smoking in this school" signs at all entrances.

1013 Find A Way To Exercise. Professionals can be more inviting when they maintain their own physical health. Whether it is organized (bowling, tennis, golf, aerobics, or racketball) or an individual effort (jogging, long walks, weight-lifting, or gardening) find a way to maintain physical fitness.

1014 Form Positive Food Habits. When eating out, order meats that are broiled, baked, or roasted rather than fried or sautéed. Avoid a lot of calories and fat. Also, take extra helpings home rather than force yourself to eat them there. The old childhood adage "clean your plate" has probably contributed to the weight problems of many professionals.

1015 Discover A Salad Bar. Check around and locate a restaurant that provides an inexpensive luncheon salad bar. For those who are able to leave campus during lunch, an inexpensive and refreshing salad is healthful and really hits the spot.

1016 **Drink And Drain.** A simple but often overlooked way to care for oneself physically is to make the rule to never pass a water fountain without taking a sip of water, or pass a restroom without making a visit! Flushing the system is a sound way to encourage good physical health.

1017 **Practice Behavioral Health.** Maintenance of good health and the prevention of illness and dysfunction can be encouraged by:

- Exercising.
- Removing salt shakers from the table.
- Avoiding high cholesterol foods.
- Fastening seat belts.
- Eliminating smoking.
- Visiting dentists regularly.
- Visiting your physician for regular physical examinations.

1018 **Make Exercise Fun.** In any school the wellness committee can encourage faculty and staff to exercise by giving funny names to various programs. For example, Mrs. Smith's (the Principal) "Smithereen Club," or Coach Jones (Head Coach) "Rat Race." Coming up with humorous names increases participation in exercise programs.

1019 **Head For The Freight Depot.** A fun activity for the social committee is to surprise the faculty at a meeting by loading everyone on a bus and taking them to the nearest truck weighing station. Get everyone to stand on the scales together, and then declare that by a certain date "We will lose a teacher." Challenge another school and send them doughnuts!

1020 **Create A Healthy Faculty Lounge.** There are many things that can contribute to good health in the faculty lounge or workroom. For example, make sure the drink machines include natural juices. Get rid of junk food machines and *insist* on a smoke-free environment.

1021 **Make A Lifelong Commitment.** Wellness is not something one does over a short time, like a diet. Make a lifelong commitment to wellness, to make healthy choices, and to assume responsibility for what you do. For example, morning exercise can become as much of a habit as going to the bathroom.

1022 **Take-A-Walk-About.** Sitting increases pressure on the spine by about forty percent. For those in school who spend a lot of time sitting, have them make it a habit to get up and walk around at every opportunity.

1023 **Walk On The Far Side.** Rather than taking the parking spot closest to the school, get in the habit of parking some distance away. The two walks a person takes each day will add to his or her wellness quotient.

1024 **Muffle The Chairs.** Used tennis balls can be cut and placed on the legs of chairs to muffle the noise in some rooms.

Postscript

So now we end this journey together. Should your energies and enthusiasm permit, we would be pleased and honored if you would take a few minutes to write us at the following addresses and share your ideas about this treasury and its future editions.

William Watson Purkey, Ed.D., NCC
Department of Counseling and Educational Development
UNC Greensboro
Greensboro, NC 27412
FAX: (910) 334–5060

Paula Helen Stanley, Ph.D., LPC
Department of Counselor Education
Radford University
Radford, VA 24142
FAX: (703) 831–6053

Bibliography

Amos, L., Smith, C., & Purkey, W. W. (1985). *Invitational teaching survey (ITS)*. UNC Greensboro, Greensboro, NC: International Alliance For Invitational Education.

Lehr, J. B., & Martin, C. (1992). *We're all at risk: Inviting learning for everyone*. Minneapolis,MN: Educational Media Corporation.

Novak, J. M. (Ed.) (1992). *Advancing invitational thinking*. San Francisco, CA: Caddo Gap Press.

Purkey, W. W. (1970). *Self concept and school achievement*. Englewood Cliffs, NJ: Prentice-Hall, Inc.

Purkey, W. W., Gage, B, & Fahey, M. (1975). *The Florida Key: An instrument to measure student self-concept-as-learner.* Greensboro, NC: International Alliance For Invitational Education, UNC Greensboro. (Revised 1993 by Paula Helen Stanley and William Watson Purkey).

Purkey, W. W., & Novak, J. M. (1984). *Inviting school success A self concept approach to teaching 2nd Edition*. Belmont, CA: Wadsworth.

Purkey, W. W., & Novak, J. M. (1988). *Education: By invitation only.* Bloomington, IN: Phi Delta Kappa Fastback.

Purkey, W. W., & Schmidt, J. J. (1990). *Invitational learning for counseling and development*. Ann Arbor, MI: ERIC/CAPS.

Purkey, W. W., & Strahan, D. (1986). *Positive discipline: A pocketful of ideas*. Columbus, OH: National Middle Schools Association.

Purkey, W. W., & Stanley, P. H. (1991). *Invitational teaching, learning and living*. Washington, DC: NEA.

Schmidt, J. J. (1988). *Invitation to friendship*. Minneapolis, MN: Educational Media Corp.

Schmidt, J. J. (1990). *Living intentionally and making life happen.* Cary, NC: Brookcliff.

Walz, G., & Bleuer, J. (1992). *Student self-esteem.* (Vol. 1) Ann Arbor, MI: ERIC/CAPS.

Wilson, J. (1986). *The invitational elementary classroom.* Springfield, IL: Charles C. Thomas.

Index